Low-Fat Love

Social Fictions Series

Series Editor
Patricia Leavy
USA

The *Social Fictions* series emerges out of the arts-based research movement. The series includes full-length fiction books that are informed by social research but written in a literary/artistic form (novels, plays, and short story collections). Believing there is much to learn through fiction, the series only includes works written entirely in the literary medium adapted. Each book includes an academic introduction that explains the research and teaching that informs the book as well as how the book can be used in college courses. The books are underscored with social science or other scholarly perspectives and intended to be relevant to the lives of college students—to tap into important issues in the unique ways that artistic or literary forms can.

Please email queries to pleavy7@aol.com

International Editorial Advisory Board

Carl Bagley, University of Durham, UK
Anna Banks, University of Idaho, USA
Carolyn Ellis, University of South Florida, USA
Rita Irwin, University of British Columbia, Canada
J. Gary Knowles, University of Toronto, Canada
Laurel Richardson, The Ohio State University (Emeritus), USA

Low-Fat Love

Expanded Anniversary Edition

Patricia Leavy

SENSE PUBLISHERS
ROTTERDAM / BOSTON / TAIPEI

A C.I.P. record for this book is available from the Library of Congress.

ISBN 978-94-6209-990-6 (paperback)
ISBN 978-94-6209-991-3 (hardback)
ISBN 978-94-6209-992-0 (e-book)

Published by: Sense Publishers,
P.O. Box 21858, 3001 AW Rotterdam, The Netherlands
https://www.sensepublishers.com/

Printed on acid-free paper

PRAISE FOR LOW-FAT LOVE

"Sometimes, when I read an especially wonderful book I say to myself, "I wish I had written that!" And that is how I feel about *Low-Fat Love*. To write a page-turner of a book that teaches about contemporary gender relationships is a major feat. Patricia Leavy has done that with *Low-Fat Love*. Truth be told, I love *Low-Fat Love* because it creates a fictional world that mirrors the gendered one we live in. I can identify with all the different characters and their issues. I would love to be in any college class or book group that was fortunate enough to be reading and discussing it. Brilliant!" **Laurel Richardson, Ph.D., The Ohio State University**

"Patricia Leavy writes with passion, verve and skill. I loved the first edition of LFL, but this expanded edition exceeded my expectations. I would run, not stroll, to get a copy for yourself and all of the important people in your life. I will use this in my relational communication and women's studies classes because it is beautiful, relatable, and offers smart critique of how pop-culture's expectations for intimate relationships often lets us down. Leavy offers readers a way to think through their close relationships and demand better of themselves and others." **Sandra L. Faulkner, Ph.D., Bowling Green State University**

"I couldn't put it down! *Low-Fat Love* is a remarkable novel that every women's studies class and interpersonal class would do well to read. The title is indicative of the search for meaningful, deep, enriching relationships beyond the artificial, low-fat love that is all too pervasive in society today. I wholeheartedly recommend this book." **Robin Patric Clair, Ph.D., Purdue University**

"My students LOVE the book. One keeps saying, 'I feel as if I am inside this story ... so colorful, so contemporary!'" **Jeasik Cho, Ph.D., University of Wyoming**

"*Low-Fat Love* is absolutely brilliant. This new edition is a must-read for anyone who has lived, loved, dreamed, and at times, settled for less than what we deserve – in other words, this is a book for everyone. Get it now, set it on your course reading lists, and give it away for birthday and holiday gifts. It will change the way you think about identity, the media and popular culture, gender, communication, feminism, education, emotion, relationships, and the sociology of human being-ism." **Anne Harris, Ph.D., Monash University and Australian Research Fellow in Creativity and Arts in Education**

"More than anything, *Low-Fat Love* proves the astonishing talent that Leavy possesses as both a writer and social commentator. This novel manages to synthesize years of research without ever feeling researched, and teaches so much without the reader feeling as if they were being educated. It's a novel that appeals to multiple audiences, and I know that many of my students, both male and female, recommended this novel to their friends and siblings for the fun enlightenment they gained. In short, read it now. You definitely won't be disappointed. It manages to be a short, 'can't put it down' book to read on the beach or on a plane, while still inspiring the sort of reflection usually reserved for self-help novels and sociology tomes. A wonderful and inspiring read that I will be using for years to come. Every student should read this book." **U. Melissa Anyiwo, Ph.D., Curry College**

"This book is a great read. Leavy writes characters that you care about. I read this book over a weekend, barely able to put it down. The story is well-developed, fun, and has great pacing. What makes this book particularly interesting is the way that Leavy, a sociologist with expertise in gender studies, weaves the findings of her social research into the story. She makes sociology accessible to a wide audience. A pioneer in arts-based research, Leavy transcends traditional academic writing to engage a variety of audiences. As a sociology professor myself, I am using this book in my Introductory Sociology course, not only to springboard discussions about gender identity and women's roles, but also to demonstrate the power of sociology beyond the classroom." **Jessica Smartt Gullion, Ph.D., Texas Woman's University**

"Based on my students' responses and my own enjoyment of the novel, I highly recommend it!" **Barbara Gurr, Ph.D., University of Connecticut**

"The characters are deep and complex, the storyline intertwined, and I couldn't put it down." **Linnea Rademaker, Ph.D., Northcentral University**

"I use *Low-Fat Love* in my Sociology of Gender and Sociological Theory courses. My students and I enjoy reading the text. The students repeatedly tell me in their reviews that reading this book is one of their favorite parts of the class; they find the material relevant and helpful for understanding sociological concepts in an accessible way. If you are looking for a fun read and/or a supplement to your gender courses, I suggest *Low-Fat Love*!" **Cheryl Llewellyn, Stony Brook University**

Also from Patricia Leavy

American Circumstance

Gender & Pop Culture
A Text-Reader
Edited by Adrienne Trier-Bieniek and Patricia Leavy

For more information, visit the author's website
www.patricialeavy.com

Pamela DeSantis, this is for you

TABLE OF CONTENTS

TABLE OF CONTENTS

ACKNOWLEDGMENTS

First and foremost, thank you Peter de Liefde, publisher extraordinaire, for your willingness to innovate and support creativity. I am forever grateful to you and the entire team at Sense Publishers, particularly Paul Chambers for your tireless marketing efforts and Jolanda Karada for your production assistance. Thank you to the editorial advisory board members of the *Social Fictions* series for your ingenuity, generosity, and support. Heartfelt thanks to Shalen Lowell, the world's best assistant, without you laboring behind the scenes none of this would be possible. Thank you to Clear Voice editing for the phenomenal copyediting services. Mr. Shuman, I was so fortunate to be in your English class in high school. Thank you! Monique Robitaille, mind-body guru goddess, thank you for making me stronger. Tori Amos, for this book I walked through the fire and "made my own Pretty Hate Machine." Deepest gratitude to the many women who have shared their stories with me over the years, both before I wrote this novel and in the years since the first edition was released. Profound appreciation to the professors who have used this novel in their courses. Special thanks to those who gave it a jumpstart: Melissa Anyiwo, Emily Barko, Jeasik Cho, Jessica Smartt Gullion, Cheryl Llewellyn, Nancy La Monica, Lauren Sardi, Meaghan Stiman, and Adrienne Trier-Bieniek. Sincere apologies and thanks to anyone whom I have forgotten to name. My gratitude to all those who have offered praise for the book. My appreciation to those in the media who took the time to talk with me when the first edition was released. These pages are also peopled with the ghosts of relationships past, and I am thankful to all those who haunt the pages. I have learned from each of you. I am also grateful to my close female friends whose humor and wisdom make their way onto these pages – you know who you are. Ally Field, as always, thank you for being my person. Celine Boyle, thank you for understanding my "real" and fictional realities and making them both better. Thank you also to the best in-laws one could hope for, Carolyn and Charles Robins. Love to Vanessa and Michaela, may you never settle for low-fat love. Of course, thank you to my great loves, Madeline and Mark: your love is the real-deal, full-fat, and allows me to live a big life! Finally, Pamela DeSantis, this is for you. Thank you for embracing our family when we moved to Maine and adorning me in Honey Tribe jewelry. You are such a warm, talented, smart person – beautiful on the inside and out. Never settle, because you deserve the real deal. Love your guts!

A STATEMENT FROM SENSE PUBLISHERS

In early 2011, Patricia approached me with the idea for a series of books written in literary forms but grounded in scholarly research, theories, and concepts, titled *Social Fictions*. With arts-based approaches to research and critical pedagogy on the rise, we saw this as an innovative way to represent and share the products of research and an opportunity to expand the bounds of academic publishing. At Sense Publishers we are committed to creativity, critical pedagogy, and new approaches to academic publishing. As the fastest-growing international publisher of books in educational research, the *Social Fictions* series naturally aligned with our mission.

Low-Fat Love, the launch title, was released in the summer of 2011 and quickly became our best-selling book. It is rare to have the privilege of publishing a book that changes the field, blurs academic and trade publishing, and ultimately becomes a landmark text. *Low-Fat Love* has done all of this while becoming a beloved cult classic in several fields. We are honored to release this revised and expanded anniversary edition with new bonus content. We are sure both old and new readers will enjoy the revised novel and added content, including activities for classroom use. With this anniversary edition, Patricia continues to expand the field of arts-based research by showing how even literary forms are open to revision.

We are also proud of the *Social Fictions* series, which has become our most popular and fastest-growing series. To date, the series has published novels, plays, short story collections, poetry, and other arts-based forms by leading and emerging scholars. Like Patricia, we are committed to offering a space for new voices and the *Social Fictions* series has become a major vehicle for doing so. In 2014, The American Creativity Association honored series creator and editor Patricia Leavy with a Special Achievement Award for her "special and extraordinary advancement of arts-based research and the groundbreaking *Social Fictions* series." Thank you to the readers who have embraced these titles and the professors who incorporate them into their curriculum.

Peter de Liefde
Owner and Founder
Sense Publishers

PREFACE

Low-Fat Love unfolds over three seasons as Prilly Greene and Janice Goldwyn, adversarial editors at a New York press, experience personal change relating to the men, and absence of women, in their lives. Ultimately, each woman is pushed to confront her own image of herself, exploring her insecurities, the stagnation in her life, her attraction to men who withhold their support, and her reasons for having settled for low-fat love.

Prilly lives in between who she is and who she longs to be. Prilly falls for Pete Rice, an unemployed, ever sexy, and curiously charming aspiring graphic novelist. Prilly thinks she is finally experiencing the big life she always sought but feared was beyond her grasp because she was "in the middle" (not beautiful nor ugly, not greatly talented nor totally hopeless – someone who could work for it). Pete's unconventional, free-spirited views on relationships unsettle Prilly, ultimately causing her to unravel over the course of their on-again-off-again love affair. Meanwhile, Janice, a workaholic, feminist in-name-only editor, overburdens Prilly, her underling, with busywork and undercuts Prilly's professional identity. Janice's regimented life is set on a new course when her alcoholic father is injured in a car accident and she is forced to face her own demons.

Along with Prilly and Janice, the cast of characters' stories are interwoven throughout and eventually connect in the third and final section of the book. The offbeat characters include: Melville Wicket, Pete's awkward friend who lives one beat outside of the moment; Jacob, Melville's younger, pothead brother; Kyle Goldwyn, Janice's seventeen-year-old son who appears ordinary in every way but is actually quite extraordinary; and Tash, Kyle's wild-child, flighty, sexpot cousin who attends NYU and ends up dating Jacob. In the end, momentum builds as the characters struggle to escape the consequences of their decisions. Unexpected events cause changes in the characters that appear minor but carry significant implications for their futures.

Low-Fat Love is underscored with a commentary about female identity building and self-acceptance and how, too often, women become trapped in limited visions of themselves. Women's media is used as a signpost throughout the book in order to make visible the context in which women come to think of themselves as well as the men and women in their lives. In this respect, *Low-Fat Love* offers a critical commentary about popular culture and the social construction of femininity. Ultimately, the book explores women's identity struggles in relation to the men in their lives and how women often develop myopic images of themselves as a part of "face-saving" strategies employed to cover up shame and a learned devaluation of self. *Low-Fat Love* suggests women seek new ways to see that they are not dependent on male approval so that they will value themselves and reject degrading relationships. Moreover, as the main characters in the book learn, the most toxic relationship a woman may participate in is often with herself. So, too, the men in *Low-Fat Love* learn that one must find one's voice or suffer the consequences.

Low-Fat Love is grounded in a decade of research and teaching about gender, relationships, and popular culture, which informs the pop-feminist undertone of the book. For a decade, I conducted numerous interviews with young women about their relationships, body image, and sexual and gender identities. Additionally, I taught many college courses on the sociology of gender, critical approaches to popular culture, and human sexuality and intimacy. These courses sparked wonderful discussions with my students about identity. All of these experiences and conversations informed the writing of this book. Moreover, my own personal experiences, although fictionalized, are interwoven into the words that follow (a practice qualitative researchers refer to as autoethnography). In these ways, *Low-Fat Love* emerges out of the arts-based research movement and seeks to fictionalize and chronicle the experiences of countless interviewees, students, and friends, as well as my own experiences.

As a novel, *Low-Fat Love* can be read purely for pleasure or used in a variety of courses in women's/gender studies, sociology, psychology, popular culture, media studies, communication, qualitative research, and arts-based research. I hope the book resonates with readers and provides a springboard for self-reflection or discussion.

Patricia Leavy

PART ONE

CHAPTER 1

"'Casey bombed into town with her daily organizer.' It's the worst first line I've ever heard! I mean, you're left with this organizer, just sitting there, for no reason. You never mention something so irrelevant right in the beginning. It's awful. Nowadays everyone thinks they can write. There are no real writers anymore," he said, flinging the manuscript on Prilly's desk.

"Just real editors, right Stuart?"

"Ah, you're just soft Prilly. You can't coddle them. There's no point."

With a friendly roll of her eyes, she agreed to the inevitable. "I know, I know," she said shaking her head. "I'll tell him we can't go forward with publication."

"Good. We have to start streamlining our list. Bad writing that sells millions of copies is one thing, but unsuccessful bad writing is an embarrassment. I don't have to remind you that we can't afford the drain."

Prilly smiled, thinking his remark about unsuccessful bad writing was dead-on. "Got it. I'll take care of it."

Stuart left her small, drab office, inadvertently knocking a teetering stack of mail off the corner of her desk. The piles on her desk taunted her. She desperately desired to have everything organized and in its place, but she just couldn't manage it for more than a couple of days at a time. She had seen an episode of Oprah where an expert said that clutter in one's office or home represented clutter in one's emotional and spiritual life. As she wondered whether that was true, she reread the beginning of the manuscript. *Is it really such a bad opening line?*

*

That night when Prilly entered her apartment she immediately kicked off her comfort heels and slipped on her at-home uniform: Old Navy black pajama pants and worn out Ugg boots. She poured a glass of

Beaujolais and lay on the couch. Remote in hand, she flipped between her usual stations and landed on *Access Hollywood*. They were featuring a story about Brad Pitt and Angelina Jolie. She always bought tabloids when they were on the cover. Although she despised the idea that they were mostly adored for their good looks, she was fascinated. Sometimes she fantasized about what Angelina's life was like. More than any other celebrity, Angelina seemed to have it all. She was ridiculously gorgeous, the kind of beauty that doesn't seem to go out of style or age. She had lived a wild life, and now she had a massive, multicultural family (that she probably never had to take care of with all her nannies, assistants, and so forth), a fabulous partner who undoubtedly worshipped her, and an amazing career. Somehow she had managed to be both an artist and a commercial success, or at least she could reasonably claim to be both. People admired her. People like Prilly. As Prilly watched the story she felt a familiar storm cloud of envy, longing, and self-loathing.

Access Hollywood was just the prelude to whatever "movie of the week" she could find. Tonight she was watching a Lifetime movie about a woman who worked as a newspaper reporter and, while reporting on a local crime, became the next target of a psychopath. As Prilly picked up each forkful of the vegetable stir-fry she made during the commercials, she couldn't help but think, *In some ways the reporter is lucky. At least her life is exciting.*

Prilly lived in between who she was and who she wanted to be. She had moved to Manhattan from Boston in search of a *big life*. She had always felt she was meant to have a big life. To date, she had barely lived a small life. Although she was an atheist, she blamed God for all her problems (when she wasn't blaming her parents). She thought it all came down to looks, to genetics. She was convinced that beautiful people have a much greater shot at a big life. Ugly people have no shot. People somewhere in the middle, which is where she was firmly located, had to work hard for it, but it *was* possible. So ever since Prilly was about seven years old and she realized that she was regular looking at best, she blamed God and her parents for her lot in life. As a teenager, she admired the beautiful, popular girls. To her, they had been graced with the best gift of all: the gift of possibility. When you are beautiful, all you have to do is add on to that to get what you want, to be who you want to be. When you aren't beautiful, you spend your life making up for it, filling in what is lacking. Compensating. At times Prilly even envied the ugly girls. If you are ugly and know it, you have no hope for a big life. Ultimately, that could be very freeing. You could focus on being content with your life as it is. Ugly girls don't have to waste time or money with makeup, hair care, exercise, beauty treatments, and fashion. What's the point? No one fabulous would ever get close enough to reject them, so they must be free from disappointment too, she thought –once they accepted their situation, at least. The ones who had it the worst were those in the middle, the girls who, with enough work, could be considered pretty but never beautiful. Those girls could taste the big life, they could see it close enough to want it, to reach for it. Prilly was in the middle.

*

Pete Rice picked up the latest Neil Gaiman book, planning to spend the next several hours reading while drinking dark roast coffee. He loved the smell of coffee brewing. It was his favorite smell.

Waiting for the coffee to brew, he replayed the scene of Rachel storming out of his apartment the night before. He decided not to call her; he didn't care. He had a theory about women. If they loved you, you could control them. If they loved you too much, it was a disaster. He had many disasters. (There was Alice, who showed up to a party at his friend's house, plastered, shouting that he had an STD. He didn't. Then there was the catalogue model, Georgia, who slashed his vintage T-shirt collection and trashed his apartment. This, of course, brings to mind Sophie, who upon catching him in bed with Georgia, used his dirty clothes to make a bonfire on the fire escape outside of his apartment. Worst of all was Sadie, who would stake out his usual haunts – a local teahouse, a sandwich shop, a pub – waiting to see him arm-in-arm with another woman. This would cause her to scream publicly as if the world was burning and only she could see it. Interestingly, this would cause the woman currently with Pete, in her guiltiest of thoughts, to want him even more.)

Pete's days depended primarily on three factors: whether or not he was screwing someone steadily (steadily for him being a long series of intense relationships that lasted about two months each), whether or not he had been out all night (he had a penchant for dance clubs, though at thirty-eight he was nearly two decades older than everyone else there), and whether or not he was working (although he resisted any kind of long-term commitment or "career" that would interfere with his art, he did take very occasional part-time jobs doing things like telemarketing or working in a one-hour photo shop, which also never lasted for more than two months). He vacillated between feeling invincible (he had an unknown genius complex, one that was imprinted with the arrogance of a guy who was better looking than behaved) and feeling utterly depressed. That day, Pete had expected to be alone.

His studio apartment consisted of one small room that served as his bedroom and workspace, a kitchenette with a cutout wall that looked into the bedroom, and a small hallway that led to the bathroom and front door. The main room had two large windows, one of which led out to a small fire escape that he used as a teeny tiny porch. Sometimes he grew pot out there, but his neighbors usually stole it.

He used an old queen-size mattress and box spring, but no bed frame, so his bed was low to the floor. Gaiman book in hand, he propped two pillows against the white stucco wall and sat down in his black and white checkered boxers and old David Bowie T-shirt. He placed his oversized "I Love NY" mug on the cinderblock to the right of his bed and opened the book. He always read the dedication first. He felt you could learn everything about the soul of an author by reading the dedication page and thus, the soul of the book. Books without dedications always disappointed him. As he flipped to the first page, there was a knock on his front door.

He walked to the door and shouted, "Who is it?"
"Melville."
Pete opened the door. Neither said a word, and Pete just walked back down his narrow hallway to his bedroom while pulling at a wedgie. Melville locked the door and followed. Pete plopped down on his mattress and picked up his coffee. Melville pulled out

the rolling computer chair tucked under the desk opposite the bed. He turned it to face Pete and sat down. Then he stood up, took off his jacket, and sat down again, placing the orange garment across his lap.

"So what's up?"

"Oh, nothing, I was downtown visiting my cousin so I thought I'd stop in. I thought that maybe we could get some coffee or something. What are you doing?"

"Nothing. I got the new Gaiman book and I was just going to start it."

"I could have gotten you a deal on that. I hope you didn't pay full price, not for the hardcover. I know a store where you can get hard covers half-off, even new ones. If you get 'em used you can get them for a few bucks. Hard covers are a rip-off anyway."

As Melville spoke, slowly as ever, Pete wished that he would shut up. He was the cheapest person he had ever met. He had holes in his sweaters and had sported the same worn-out, ugly, orange windbreaker for the whole time Pete had known him – more than a decade. Pete hated going out to eat with him because Melville refused to tip appropriately. He left spare change, usually about a four percent tip at most. Pete was cheap too, but only privately. In public, he intentionally gave the impression of being generous, but in private, he often screwed friends who loaned him money, haggled with the landlord over the rent if any minor repair was needed (real or imagined), and while he always had money for expensive restaurants, liquor, books, art supplies, and all things entertainment, he never seemed to have money for anything else. For example, he had no health, dental, or life insurance. Nor did he have any property beyond the books and odds and ends in his tiny rented apartment. He routinely bought an overpriced cappuccino from the café down the street, only to drink a sip and forget about it, but he couldn't manage to pay his utilities on time and consistently ended up paying late fees and even reinstallation charges. As the flaws in others are always much more apparent than those in ourselves, Pete was oblivious. He wished that Melville wasn't so cheap or at least that he'd have the good sense to shut up about it. The truth was that he was embarrassed to be friends with Melville. Pete prided himself on chasing the muse, being in tune with the zeitgeist, and living in the moment. To Pete,

Melville was the embodiment of all that he disdained. Pete decided that Melville lived one beat outside the moment. That was why he was so slow to relay the simplest of information and why, at the age of thirty-six, Pete suspected he might still be a virgin. Yet despite his harsh evaluation of Melville, he remained the only reliable presence in Pete's life.

Totally ignoring Melville's inane hardcover commentary, Pete shot back with, "Yeah, ok, let's go grab a bite. I need to shower. You can make yourself some coffee if you want. I'm out of filters but there's paper toweling there. Flip through that book, or look in that folder over there," he said, pointing to a pile of papers on the desk behind Melville. "I've expanded the carnival part of the story and I'd like to know what you think. No one's read it yet. You're in for a treat. I'll be out in a jiff," Pete hollered as he walked to the bathroom, coffee mug in hand.

Forty-five minutes later, they were sitting down in a diner three blocks away. Pete was an inconsistent regular. He went through spurts of eating there nearly every day, sometimes more than once a day, but then he didn't go for months at a time. Just as the waitresses were getting to know him, he took a hiatus and they had forgotten him by the time he returned. When the waitress came to take their order, Pete couldn't help but notice how unusual looking she was. He had a knack for noticing atypical faces, and this face intrigued him. It was fairly old but probably appeared older than its biological age. It had very long features and a strong nose. After further examination he determined that the nose was in fact so ugly that he actually found it quite wonderful. He expected an interesting accent to match the face, but when she said, "What'll it be?" it was with the same New York accent he had come to tire of during the last five of the fifteen years he had been in the States.

"I'll have two eggs over easy with wheat toast. I'd like marmalade on the side, not jam. And coffee, with cream."

"And you?" she asked looking at Melville, who was still staring directly into the oversized plastic laminated menu.

"Um, what does the special egg sandwich come with?"

"Home fries."

"Does it come with a drink?"

"No, just home fries."

"Um, ok, I'll have that."

"Something to drink?"

"Just water."

Pete, growing tired of these uncomfortable exchanges, occupied himself by doodling in the small notepad he always carried. By the time Melville looked up from his menu, Pete was in another world.

"So I read the new pages."

"Yeah, and?" Pete asked, both eager to hear the response and annoyed that he had to coax it out of him.

"They're good but you're missing some commas in a couple of places. I can show you where." (Melville had been an English major in college, until he dropped out sophomore year.)

"Commas? Fucking commas? This is your insight? I don't give a fuck about commas! I hate fucking commas. Do you have anything useful to contribute or are you just taking up space?"

Although hurt by Pete's patronizing rant, Melville ignored it, as he was accustomed to doing. Wanting to show Pete he had more to offer, that he wasn't just "taking up space," he quickly retorted, "Well I don't get where you are going with the main character. The writing is good but there's nowhere to take it."

"Ha! You should stick to commas," Pete said through hearty laughter.

Melville shrugged, looking down. Although Pete didn't notice, Melville never looked him in the eyes. Never. He normally looked down and sometimes to the side.

"You'll get it when it's all there. That's your problem, you need it all spelled out. Can't feeeeel where it's headin'. But don't worry, it'll all be there and you'll get it."

With that, the waitress brought their breakfast. Melville ate swiftly, looking down at his food the entire time. Pete spent a few minutes dunking the corner of his toast into his egg yolks before eating.

At the end of the meal, there was some typical squabbling about the bill. Melville left his usual four percent tip. Anyone else would have just thrown some extra money down, but Pete, being secretly cheap himself, guilt-tripped Melville into putting down a couple of dollars. Pete either didn't realize or didn't care that when Melville gave in it was just to get him to shut up. Melville couldn't stand the sound of Pete's voice. Although he envied him, particularly with women, he also found Pete laborious. Walking out, Pete noticed a flyer in the entrance of the diner. It announced a book reading by Jeanette Winterson that Saturday afternoon at a local bookstore. He ripped down the flyer and said, "We should go to this. It would be good for you to hear the work of a real writer. No one uses metaphor quite like Winterson. She's good."

Not acknowledging the condemnation, Melville simply replied, "Yeah, ok."

*

On the train, Melville Wicket sat still and silent. Weeks earlier he moved into his younger brother Jacob's apartment in Brooklyn, which he shared with a manic-depressive named Jeremy.

Melville was a telemarketer for a medical insurance company. He only worked twenty-eight hours a week so his employer could avoid paying him benefits, like medical insurance. With hardly enough income to live, Melville had been staying in a small basement room in a rooming house for the past three years. He paid month-to-month. Some residents had week-to-week deals. The room was half above ground and half below. There were two small rectangular windows high on the right wall, nearly touching the ceiling, with rusty iron bars. Underneath the windows was a small refrigerator, the kind you would expect to find in a college dorm room, a microwave, and an electric Crock-Pot that violated building codes. Across from the windows was a twin bed with old, off-white sheets, one flattened pillow, and a worn out, queen sized down comforter with a few holes. Sometimes when Melville woke up in the morning, there were feathers in his hair. In his mind, he called them *chicken feathers*. To the left of the bed was a small, unfinished wooden desk and brown leather chair. On the desk, he kept a stack of library books, a few pieces of old mail, notebooks and pens, an old word processor from 1995, and a small alarm clock with a CD player. On the floor beneath, stacks of CDs. To the right, a tall halogen lamp. There was a shared bathroom in the hallway. Melville was allotted one shelf in the medicine cabinet for his personal items, which he used, although he didn't feel good about it.

Melville would have stayed there forever, but was asked to leave at the end of the previous month. One of the female residents complained to the super that Melville had been peeping on her while she was in the bathroom. She reported that she saw him through the slit of the barely-opened door, a door she claimed to have closed. He must have pushed ever so slightly open, she had argued. Two years earlier, another woman had made a similar complaint. Melville denied it, in his usual quiet manner. The super took pity on him and let him stay, but now with a second complaint, he was out. When he told Pete what happened, Pete said, "Spying? You were spying on the girls? Ha!" Melville insisted he hadn't done it, but Pete rolled his eyes and didn't say anything else. He always assumed that Melville was guilty, not because he was a pervert, but because he was shy, and awkward, and terribly lonely.

Jacob hadn't wanted Melville to move in with him, but what could he do? The guy was basically homeless, and he *was* his brother. Besides, he could get money for rent and utilities, leaving more money for pot and the occasional celebratory mushroom. Jacob was twenty-four and worked in what he called a "vintage music store" in the Village, near Washington Square Park. The store sold rare vinyl and used CDs, dealing largely in trade. Melville wondered how a store like that could stay in business in the age of eBay and iTunes. He once asked Jacob about it and was told to "shut the fuck up." Melville never mentioned it again. Melville didn't know what Jeremy did for a living. Most days he stayed in his room all day, sleeping, Melville assumed. But every Tuesday, he was up and out of the house by eight o'clock and didn't return until after six in the evening. Melville didn't ask questions.

After spending the morning with Pete, Melville returned to his apartment at three o'clock. He went straight into his small bedroom. It was actually a two-bedroom apartment with a small living and kitchenette combo room and one tiny bathroom with a stall shower. The apartment also had a very small sunroom that Jacob turned into a makeshift bedroom for his brother. With no room for a bed, Melville slept on a small couch. The room was very drafty, and Melville was worried about winter. He thought about it all the time. On that day, as most, he entered his room, took off his sneakers, and put on a Puccini CD. He lay on his couch with his jacket still on, listening.

*

Prilly's search for a big life hadn't amounted to much. She was in her office from eight until six-thirty every weekday. By the time she got back to her apartment, it was time for *Access Hollywood* and a healthy dinner, followed by a bad junk food binge with a side of guilt and a movie about women who steal other women's babies or who murder their young repairmen lovers. Although she had been in New York for several years, she hadn't managed to make more than a couple of friends, and she didn't really like them. Much like the fat girl in high school whom she befriended, this, for now, was the best she could do. The single women at work routinely went to local bars together, and, although they always invited her, she never once went. She felt uncomfortable and feared it would be awful. After a while, she noticed that they didn't actually invite her, but rather said, "We're heading to Maxwell's." She assumed she was welcome to join them, or else why would they bother to announce where they were going. But she wasn't sure.

She took one stab at Internet dating. The Internet appealed to her for two main reasons. First, no one had to know about it, so if it didn't work out, she wouldn't have to explain her failure to anyone. Second, she could screen the men based on income, education, looks, and interests. She wanted a man who earned more money than she did, not because she had any intention of becoming dependent on a man, but because it would be hard to have a big life in Manhattan without more money, and a lot of it. She also wanted to get out from under her mounting credit card debt, which weighed on her, particularly on the nights she drank excessively. She hoped to meet someone interested in the arts, who could take her to the best shows. Although she wanted to be with a good-looking man, which she believed made a so-so looking woman seem much more attractive, she didn't want to be with a man that was too good looking. Men like that always left average women eventually. It was hard to fool them into thinking you were prettier than you actually were. If she managed to get a decent man and turn it into a steady thing, she didn't want to have to do it all over again someday. She also feared being part of a couple that made other women wonder: *What is he doing with her?*

The Internet dating ended up costing her $199, a weekend's worth of screening time, one terrible evening, and an untold sum of shame. She had made a date with Henry. He seemed promising. He was an accountant who owned his own apartment and claimed to see every foreign film that came out. They planned to meet at a Spanish tapas restaurant a few blocks from her office for a drink and quick bite. She thought about the date incessantly for five days. She got a manicure, bikini wax, and bought two new outfits (neither of which she wore; she decided one was weird and the other looked too "datey"). On the night they were supposed to meet, she got to the restaurant, stood outside for a minute panicking, walked around the block, and then decided that if he had seen her walk around the block he would already think she was a freak. She went home, drank nearly a bottle of wine, and watched four hours of a nine-hour *Murder, She Wrote* marathon on the Hallmark channel. Henry sent her an email the next morning asking what happened and if she was ok. She never responded and removed her profile from match.com immediately. She felt guilty for months, thinking of Henry often.

Without many friends to go out with and no real effort made at dating, her life was fairly lonely. She decided to invest energy into her weekend routine. Convinced that if you lead an interesting life you will meet interesting people, Prilly made being interesting her full-time weekend occupation. For her, there was nothing more interesting than the arts. Had she been braver, she might have been some sort of artist, or at least a journalist. She took to surrounding herself with the products of others' bliss. The monotony of the workweek was soon juxtaposed to weekends of ballet, theatre, concerts, gallery openings, craft markets, spoken word performances, independent films, museums, and poetry readings. It was exhausting.

*

"Well I wanted to tell you in person. I know it's difficult, but please don't take it personally. We're a mid-sized press and we need to be very careful about which books we publish, particularly for our trade market. Usually we don't even consider unsolicited works."

"But you've sold fifteen thousand copies of my last book. That should count for something. That's why I came to you first. I just don't understand this. Isn't there anything I can do?"

"Yes, I understand how you must feel," Prilly responded in a hushed tone, "but that was an introductory geography textbook. It was an academic printing with a built-in audience we could market to. If you talk with Marcy, I'm sure she can explain it to you. The trade market is very different and we publish very few new fiction authors each year. I'm sorry but we can't go with this and I don't want to waste your time. I encourage you to submit it elsewhere."

After a moment of silence, during which Prilly could hear her own breath, Charles matter-of-factly said, "Well, I'm very disappointed. Very disappointed." With that, the large, pear-shaped man got up, outstretched his arm over Prilly's desk for a sweaty handshake, and left.

Prilly felt awful. Normally she just sent rejection emails or letters. She never saw the person she was rejecting, but because Charles was already published with the house, Stuart suggested she do it in person the next time Charles stopped by to see Marcy, the geography editor.

Before Prilly could regroup, Janice popped her head in the door, left ajar by Charles. The sight of Janice made Prilly crave Advil. Janice was a long-time acquisitions editor with the press and Prilly had been her assistant for nine months before being promoted to editor. It was the longest nine months of her life. At first she thought she was incredibly lucky. She was told that there were very few women in publishing who had made it to Janice's level, with her list of accomplishments. After ten years of working in their geography division, Janice was given a new list to build, history, a market the press had never ventured into before. With a degree in history, Janice had purportedly been thrilled. She introduced herself to Prilly as a feminist. She boldly said, "Prilly, this is a male-dominated industry. It's not easy, but it *can* be done and we have to support each other." She also prided herself on including women's history and Black history in her line, books she swore other editors would forego.

Prilly soon discovered that feminism was more of an abstract concept with Janice. She really enjoyed talking about supporting "women's issues," but she didn't support *actual women*. In fact, over time Prilly learned that Janice was particularly harsh on the women she worked with out of some irrational fear that they would become more successful than her, and what's worse, that they wouldn't have to work as hard to do it. Janice had to work for everything she had, and unlike the "anorexic bitches" she went to college with, she scraped for everything she got, including her education. As a result, Janice only liked women in positions beneath her, those that she could easily manipulate and therefore control.

Janice liked Prilly well enough at first, but when she realized that Prilly wouldn't be content being an assistant forever, she grew weary. This weariness led to a quiet resentment. Prilly often found herself working outrageously long hours that mostly consisted of doing secretarial work for Janice, which was not in her job description. Assigning these kinds of tasks helped Janice on two levels. First, it made it clear to Prilly and anyone else paying attention that she was in charge, that she was Prilly's boss. Second, and even more importantly, it prevented Prilly from doing the kind of work that the publishers would notice, the kind of work that would get Prilly promoted. What Janice failed to recognize was that the publishers had always intended Prilly for an editorial position. They only made her an assistant first so the others wouldn't complain about rank jumping. When Prilly was promoted, she immediately went to Janice, hoping to avoid future unpleasantness.

"Thank you so much, Janice. Without your mentorship, this never would have happened."

"Well, actually I did put in a good word for you, too. I had to push for this. I had to make this happen. But you deserve it," Janice replied in her usual quiet and monotone voice.

Prilly thanked her although she knew it wasn't true. In fact, she suspected that Janice secretly gave her mediocre performance reviews so she would remain her assistant indefinitely. Ever since, Janice went out of her way to be nice to Prilly, so much so that it alarmed her. Once in a while, Janice found a way to say something cutting under the guise of being helpful, like the knock about having to convince the bosses to promote her. It was no wonder that the mere sight of Janice at her door caused a sharp pain in her spine.

"Hi Prilly. What was that about? Charles looked pretty upset when he left. He used to be one of my authors you know."

Prilly relaxed a bit, hoping Janice was just nosing around for gossip, as she was prone to do, and didn't want anything beyond chitchat.

"Oh, that's right. He's one of Marcy's now. Same old, same old. He's an academic who thinks he can also be a novelist. I had to tell him that his manuscript isn't for us. He took it pretty hard, but what can you do, you know."

Janice shimmied her way into the doorway, allowing her back to gently tap the door closed as if unintentionally. *Oh great*, Prilly thought. *There's more.*

"Do you want to come in and sit down?" Prilly asked entirely out of obligation.

"Oh sure, just for a minute."

Janice always had a way of making things seem like they were someone else's idea, as if *she* was doing *you* a favor.

"Prilly, I wanted to run something by you."

"Sure, what's up?"

"I want to build a list of memoirs, focusing mostly on unknown female authors."

"That sounds great, Janice. You should give Stuart a proposal."

"Well I did actually, and that's where you come in. Stuart said that memoirs would fall under your list, that they're sold as trade books and since we don't publish non-fiction trade, they'd have to be a part of our current trade list. He thought it would make sense for someone in your division to partner up with me."

"Hmmm."

"So I suggested that you and I work on it together. We could do it as a book series instead of a line, at least as a sort of pilot test. If we solicit authors who have already drafted manuscripts, we could premier at Trade Launch this spring. You and I could serve as co-editors-in-chief for the series, with my name listed first. If it does well, we could eventually build a full line. I think this would be an excellent opportunity for you."

Yeah, I bet you do, Prilly thought to herself. She learned long ago that Janice only cared about opportunities for herself. Anytime she framed something as an opportunity for someone else, Prilly thought that the poor soul should run like the wind. A part of Prilly actually liked Janice, despite all the obvious reasons not to. At times, she even thought that her fondness for Janice grew in direct proportion to her manipulative behavior. Although she was very different from Janice, deep down she knew that a part of them was the same. A part of each of them had been shafted and was clawing their way out the best way they knew how. Janice's claws were simply sharper. She also wanted to believe in Janice's tale of great feminist heroism in publishing, even though she knew it was all a lie. If Janice would just be more forthright, Prilly could even be friends with her. She kept this thought to herself.

"Well it does sound interesting. Why don't you give me your proposal? I'll look it over and we can talk more. I'm really swamped as it is, but I'll definitely look at what you have."

"I'm telling you, this is a great opportunity for you. In fact, Stuart didn't think you were up for it yet, but with my convincing, he's willing to give you a shot."

"Well I appreciate that," Prilly said, the way a child thanks their parents when they're given socks for Christmas. "It sounds like a great opportunity but I'd like to look over the specifics and think about it."

Janice couldn't conceal her irritation as she fiddled with her pin-straight, light brown hair, but she played along. "Ok, I'll email you the proposal and Stu's notes. We can talk about it early next week."

"Ok, great. Thanks, Janice."

Janice left her office, shutting the door behind her. Prilly took four Advil.

*

The weekend couldn't come fast enough for Prilly. She spent Friday night at home with half a bottle of red wine and Chinese takeout. (She always ate right out of the container with the disposable chopsticks. She thought it was more sophisticated, even though no one was there to see it, and she had no idea how to use chopsticks properly, so food invariably landed on her couch. This also prevented her from ordering the veggie fried rice she liked, since she couldn't possibly eat rice with chopsticks). On Saturday, she woke up late with a wine and MSG headache and took two Advil.

With no plans until Sunday (when she was meeting an old friend for a several-times-rescheduled lunch), she sipped her French roast while perusing one of her favorite New York websites, which listed events of interest. Jeanette Winterson was doing a book reading and signing at four o'clock. The bookstore was near the shoe repair store where she had left her silver shoes for heel reinforcement. Prilly liked to multitask. Plus, *there are sure to be interesting people at the book reading*, she thought.

CHAPTER 2

"Hang on a minute. Fuck, Melville's banging on the damn door. No, we're going to a book reading. I'm not even dressed so I'd better get movin. I'll call you later. Hang in there. Bye."

When Pete hung up the phone, he stammered down his hallway and opened the door. He turned around and walked back to the kitchenette without saying a word. Melville shut the door and followed.

"Christ, I was on the phone. Can't you wait a minute?" Pete asked with a tone that made it clear he was not looking for an answer. "I'm making coffee, do you want some?"

"No, thanks," Melville said as he grabbed a comic book off Pete's desk and sat in the chair, flipping through its pages. Melville didn't care for comic books; he thought they were juvenile and beneath him, but like so many other thoughts, he kept this to himself.

"I just need to throw my clothes on. I'll bring the coffee to go."

"Ok," Melville said as he read a random page from the middle of the comic book.

*

The bookstore was crowded, and by the time Pete and Melville arrived, fifteen minutes late (though Winterson hadn't yet begun her reading), there weren't any seats left. Melville was secretly annoyed that Pete, per usual, wasn't ready on time. They stood in the back, leaning against a wall. Pete, burnt out from a sleepless night, sipped his coffee steadily.

When Winterson appeared, everyone stood up and began clapping ferociously. She began by talking about her new work, from which she read several passages. She then took questions from the audience about her first novel, *Oranges Are Not the Only Fruit*, and fan favorites like *Sexing the Cherry*. Prilly, who sat in the corner of the back row, hadn't read any of Winterson's books, although she owned several. They were amidst the collection of "important artistic works" she thought everyone should own, and someday even read.

At the end of the question period, there was a book signing. The mob scurried to the front, forming a swerving line through the store. Prilly detested standing in lines. She also hadn't brought any books with her and wasn't committed to buying the new book. She picked up her unmarked brown paper bag that contained her newly repaired shoes and turned to head out. The bag didn't have a handle and was cumbersome. She stuck it under one of her arms and threw her handbag on her opposite shoulder. She fumbled a bit as she made her way past the rows of arranged chairs toward the door. Melville, still leaning against the wall with Pete, noticed her immediately. *She is lovely*, he thought. It was his irrepressible staring that made Pete aware of her. As Prilly walked by, Pete said, "You're not getting a book?"

"I'm sorry. Did you say something to me?" Prilly asked, catching a glimpse of Pete for the first time. He had striking teal eyes framed with a few soft lines that made her think, *he's really lived*.

"I just asked if you were getting a book, like everyone else seems to be doing."

"Oh," noticing how sexy his voice was. "The line is too long."

"My friend and I are going to get a coffee and talk about the reading. Would you like to join us?"

Stunned by the invitation from a tall, dark-haired man whose name she didn't yet know, Prilly stammered. Pete quickly responded, "It's ok, no worries, but if you're not busy, come along."

Pete walked ahead of Prilly, opened the door, and let her pass through. He then stepped outside with Melville following. He turned to Prilly, who was shocked by both the unexpected invitation and the willingness with which this man would let her just leave. "Well, have a good evening," he said as he turned and started walking down the street.

Prilly watched as he and Melville went into a café halfway down the block. She turned to walk in the other direction, but as if in slow motion, she stopped mid-movement and turned back toward the café. *I'll hate myself if I don't check this out*. When she walked into the café, Pete was sitting on a long, red velvet couch. He smiled and said, "Well, you changed your mind."

"I thought I'd just come for a quick coffee."

"Great." He jumped up and got in line next to Melville, cutting in front of several people who didn't seem to mind.

Prilly put down her brown bag and sat on a wooden chair opposite Pete's vacated spot on the couch. "What'll ya have?" he hollered.

"Oh, a cappuccino. A non-fat cappuccino, please."

They took only a minute to place the order and soon returned with drinks in hand. "Thank you," she said as Pete handed her the foamy beverage.

"My name is Pete, and this is Melville, my editor," Pete said with a smirk as he plopped down on the couch.

"I'm Prilly. Prilly Greene." Turning to Melville, who was sitting in the chair to her right, she said, "You're an editor? Me too, that's so funny. I'm at WISE. Which house are you with?"

Pete laughed and said, "The house of Jacob."

Melville stuttered a bit and Prilly, not knowing what was so funny, turned to Pete. "Are you a writer?" she asked.

"Yes. Graphic novels mostly, but I do a little of everything."
He's very sexy, too sexy for me really, but he seems interested. Prilly was disproportionately impressed by him, considering they had just met. She loved his British accent though she was embarrassed by her own trite thoughts. He immediately reminded her of the lead singer from the '80s band A-ha. She had always loved the video for their song, "Take On Me," in which the singer is transformed into a cartoon illustration who falls in love with a plain-looking diner waitress. Every time she saw that video she wondered why they didn't get a more glamorous woman to play the love interest, but she cherished the video because it gave her hope. That was exactly how she felt with Pete.

Although clearly a bit full of himself, Pete was well read and Prilly was enamored. After talking about the book reading for quite a while, they decided to go out for dinner. Prilly said that she wanted to stop at her apartment first to drop off the bag with her shoes. She actually wanted to freshen up and throw a toothbrush and some makeup in her pocketbook just in case she didn't make it home that night. Although she had no intention of sleeping with him, this was the most exciting thing that had happened to her in a long time and she wanted to be prepared for spontaneity.

Suddenly worried that she just invited two total strangers into her apartment, she felt a mix of trepidation and exhilaration as she clumsily turned the key in the lock. "I'll just be a couple of minutes. Feel free to look at those books," she said, pointing to her bookshelf before she darted into her bedroom. She returned ten minutes later with a larger handbag and without the brown paper bag that had become a source of gags on the way to her apartment. "Are you ready to go?" she asked.

"I'm going to head home. I forgot that I promised my brother I'd watch a movie with him tonight," Melville said. "He already rented it."

"Oh, ok," Prilly responded, not knowing if it was true or if Pete had asked Melville to make himself scarce so they could be alone. Though she was hoping that the latter was true, the thought also made her stomach knot. She had never been with someone so good looking before.

The three walked out together, and Melville headed left while Pete and Prilly turned right.

*

When he entered his apartment, Jacob was sitting on the couch with three guys that Melville had seen there before but had never been introduced to. They were passing around a joint and listening to some god-awful reggae music. Melville walked over to the refrigerator and took out a small bottle of Orangina and a Tupperware with leftover macaroni with meat sauce that he made a few days earlier. He popped the macaroni into the microwave. The ninety-second cooking time felt like eternity as Melville awkwardly waited for the beep. "Hey, I thought you were hanging with Pete tonight. Did he ditch you?" Jacob hollered from the couch. Suddenly, there were four sets of bloodshot eyes peering at him.

"He met a girl. Wanted to be alone with her. She's beautiful," Melville quietly said, embarrassed that, in fact, he had again been ditched. Jacob and his friends returned their focus to their joint, and Melville took his dinner into his room where he ate while listening to Stravinsky and thinking of Prilly.

*

"'Casey bombed into town with her daily organizer.' Ha! That's terrible," Pete said as his voice became higher and his laughter morphed into a cackle.

"Really? You think so? It's not Pulitzer material but I don't think it's so bad. You should have seen the guy. He looked … he looked like he was trying to pretend he wasn't shattered. He's one of our established authors. I felt really badly for him."

"You've got to be kidding. It's dreadful. That could be an example in a book about how *not* to write. Maybe you could use it for that," Pete said, again punctuating his suggestion with laughter.

Pete was bordering on hurting her feelings, and he was definitely arrogant, but she let it slide and just said, "Yeah, I guess it's pretty bad," even though she still didn't understand why.

After a two-hour dinner at the bar of a pub that Pete recommended, where they split the bill, Prilly was in Pete's apartment sharing a bottle of red wine they picked up along the way (which Prilly had paid for because Pete suddenly became fascinated by plastic lighters when it was their turn at the register). Normally Prilly would have been put off by such a scruffy little apartment, but on that night she saw the simplicity differently. *He's living like a real artist*, she thought.

With only one chair in the apartment, Pete invited her to sit on the bed. When she hesitated he said, "Don't worry, you don't have to sleep with me or anything," followed by a short burst of laughter which she was beginning to realize was a regular part of his communication.

"Oh, I know," she said uncomfortably as she went to sit on the bed, careful not to spill her wine. Wanting to change the subject, Prilly asked, "What have you written? You said something about graphic novels. I don't know much about that genre but would I know your work?"

"Oh, no. No, you wouldn't know my work. I haven't been ready to publish. Haven't sent it out anywhere. But soon."

As an editor, Prilly didn't know what to make of this. She dealt with writers every day who were desperate to publish, who wanted it more than anything else. "When you say you're not ready to publish, do you mean that you haven't completed a work or are you one of those perfectionists who wants to get it all just so before you hand it over? Because you'd be amazed by how useful copyeditors can be."

"Well, I'll put it to you this way: if I were a gardener I would have the most beautiful, unusual flowers in the most unexpected and glorious colors. Everywhere the eye darted would be unimaginable wonder. However, I wouldn't remember to water them and they would all die." He laughed. "Besides, Melville does my copyediting."

"Ah," Prilly said, choosing to ignore the warning she knew the universe might be sending her. She also chose not to ask how he earned a living. (Days later, he would tell her that he lived mainly off an inheritance from his parents who had both died young of lung cancer although neither were smokers.) Instead of making her wonder about his work ethic, she just felt sorry for him.

They moved on to childhood tales (he had stories about eating candy floss on autumn days; she had no idea what candy floss was but it sounded wonderful), his days in college (he was a philosophy major who dropped out during his third year because there was nothing more to learn from the professors), his subsequent adventures in London (where he befriended many drug-addicted counter-culture artists), and eventually his move to New York (for "the energy"). She briefly told him about how much she loved her career, but mostly she just listened. After a few hours of talking, listening to new wave music that Prilly couldn't believe she had never heard before, and flipping through folders of Pete's work that appeared to be fragmented bits of rambling sprinkled with something magical, she realized it was past midnight.

"I should probably go."

"Don't be silly, spend the night. We can go out for breakfast in the morning. There's a wonderful little diner nearby with a fabulous waitress. She has the most unusual face, you have to see it. Do you have plans tomorrow?"

Prilly did have tentative plans with her friend Yvonne, and she wasn't sure if she wanted to sleep with Pete yet, but she said, "No, no plans."

"Settled. I have only the one bed so you'll have to sleep with me but don't worry, we can just sleep. I'll get you a T-shirt to wear." Prilly went into the bathroom and put on the oversized Smiths T-shirt he had given her. She looked in the small, toothpaste-splattered mirror above the sink and wondered, *What am I doing? Thank god I brought my toothbrush.*

She timidly returned to the bed and carefully crawled in. Pete smiled at her and said, "Good night," as he flipped off the light switch. She lay awake for hours pretending to sleep.

The next morning, she heard Pete wrestling around in bed. She slowly turned to him, conscious of her morning breath. He looked her in the eyes and softly said, "Good morning."

Not wanting to breathe on him, she looked down and whispered, "Good morning." She turned around, lying with her back to him. He put his hand on her shoulder and she moved closer to him. He slid his hand under her T-shirt and rubbed her breasts. Then he moved his hands down and gently pulled her panties off. He put his hand on her and started slowly motioning. He slid into her and they made love, never turning to each other, never kissing.

CHAPTER 3

After blowing off her friend with a text message in order to spend the rest of the weekend with Pete, Prilly floated into her office Monday feeling exhilarated. Even though she knew Pete probably wasn't terribly successful, all she could think about was how sexy he was and how lucky she was to have met him. Filled with excitement over plans to see him that evening, and wearing her lucky bronze colored slingback heels, Prilly barely noticed when Janice popped into her doorway before she even had a chance to turn on her computer.

"It's nine fifteen. You're always here right at eight o'clock. I was concerned. A little bit longer and I would have called you just to make sure you were ok."

Considering they had almost no relationship whatsoever, she wondered why Janice was feigning concern for her. That thought temporarily distracted her from wondering why Janice was keeping tabs on what time she got into the office.

"Oh, I had a late night, so I decided to come in a little later today," Prilly said, suddenly realizing it was none of Janice's business.

Too focused on her own agenda to recognize an opportunity to prod for more information, Janice simply asked, "Well, what do you think?"

"About what?"

This caused Janice to roll her eyes, flip her hair, and sigh all at once. Prilly was worried she might hurt herself. She hijacked the chair facing Prilly and responded sharply, "About the memoir series."

"Oh, right. I'm so sorry, but I was really busy this weekend and I didn't have a chance to look over the materials. Can I get back to you later in the week?"

"Prilly, this is really an excellent opportunity and it's time sensitive. We need to get moving on this."

Time sensitive? Prilly wondered to herself. *It's not that time sensitive.* But she realized that Janice was fixated and would be relentless. If Prilly ultimately turned her down, Janice would be out to get her, and may not be subtle about it any longer. If she agreed to work with Janice, she would probably end up suicidal. It was a toss-up. Feeling invincible from the two orgasms she had the night before, Prilly decided that with her personal life taking this wonderfully unexpected turn, it wouldn't be such a bad time to take on a new work challenge. Maybe the series would be a hit. Memoirs were interesting. Best yet, Pete would be impressed.

"Well, I still want to review the materials in order to under-stand the scope of the commitment and what the compensation will be, but I think it's a good idea. I'd like to do it with you."

"Great! This is a terrific opportunity for you. I mean, I don't really have time for it either, but I think it will really strengthen our line and help your career." As Prilly was contemplating this last remark, Janice stood up and smiled. "I'll let Stu know. Let's set up a meeting later this week to go over the details and draft our work plan." Janice turned on her heel and left Prilly's office, closing the door behind her. Prilly worried about what she had just gotten herself into.

*

That night, feeling good about cajoling Prilly into the memoir series, Janice arrived home at a quarter to eight with a canvas bag of groceries hanging on one shoulder and her maroon leather laptop case in her hand. She hurriedly entered her house as the grocery bag started slipping. From the kitchen she shouted, "Richard, are you home?" as she unpacked green grapes, sliced turkey, wheat rolls, and three bottles of Pellegrino sparkling water. To break the silence she hollered, "Kyle, Kyle please come here." Nothing. *He's probably out with his friends again,* she thought. After making a turkey sandwich with a slather of Miracle Whip, the one taste of her childhood in which she found comfort, she flung her canvas bag on the coat rack near the front door, grabbed the computer case she had abandoned there, and headed into the dining room, which over time had become her office. Sitting alone at the end of a long, rectangular, dark mahogany table covered with stacks of manila folders and books, she took out her folder labeled "Ideas for the Memoir Series" and started to work. The sandwich sat untouched beside her.

*

Janice Goldwyn prided herself on three things: her career, her family, and her house. More accurately, she prided herself on the appearance of her career, the idea of her family, and while she truly loved her house, she always feared that she best not get too comfortable there. So she didn't.

Growing up, Janice didn't have much. She lived on the outskirts of Detroit. Her father was a nasty drunk. Janice desperately wanted his approval, so she worked her absolute hardest in school. Each afternoon, she came bounding into the house where she found him half reclined in his old sky blue Lazy Boy, drinking a beer and watching *Family Feud*. She gently tapped him on the shoulder (after learning not to jump right in front of him, thus obstructing his view). He always ignored her. Unable to contain her enthusiasm she happily said, "Pop, Pop, guess what? I got an A on my geography test," or, "Pop, Pop, guess what? Miss Murphy hung my painting up in art class," or, "Pop, Pop, I beat my obstacle course record in gym class. Maybe I can be a Marine like you someday."

To her excitement and accomplishments, her father always had the same response: "Biiiig nothing. Scatter. Scatter you pissant." Unlike Janice's younger sister, Marge, who despised their father and didn't care what he thought, Janice never stopped trying. Day after day, year after year, this scene repeated. Over time, Janice came to resent her mother, Myra. Janice saw their situation as her mother's fault. She thought her mother must be inadequate, weak, a loser. When she hung all of Janice's crayon drawings on their refrigerator, Janice concluded that she was too easily impressed. After long days at a factory clear across town, four bus rides, two there and two back, cooking, cleaning, sewing, and countless other acts of sheer survival, Myra inevitably had to face the lifeless eyes of a pathetic drunk and the scorn-filled eyes of her daughter, who looked at Myra as if *she* were the pathetic one. A quiet, devout Catholic who believed her duty to her family disavowed her of the perils of wants of her own, she took it. She took it all, without request or complaint.

Janice grew both ambitious and resentful. Her efforts to impress her father resulted in acceptance to seven high-ranking colleges, all of which were conveniently located far away from Detroit. She found it impossible to make friends in college. She had two part-time jobs (a scholarship and student loans paid for the rest). One job was as a research assistant, which actually meant errand girl, but she told her sister in weekly phone calls that it was "important work that would be published." She also worked at the check-in station at the school fitness center, where she watched the "spoiled bitches and dumbass jocks" hang out while she read Proust or Dostoyevsky, always for a class, never for pleasure.

When she wasn't working, she was studying, regularly pulling all-nighters. One night, as she fought sleep at her desk while trying to get through Adam Smith's economic theory, she pulled a yellow post-it note off her pad and wrote, "I'll sleep when I'm dead." She stuck it to her desk and used it for motivation. Anything less than an A devastated her. This often prompted her to offer to rewrite papers and do extra credit assignments. If professors told her "grades weren't everything," she instantly detested them. Her initial sweet tone darkened and she accused them of "low balling" her.

Her schedule wasn't the reason she didn't have friends. She resented the other students so intensely that she mistook the smallest politeness for veiled criticism, often causing her to say something cutting and totally unwarranted. For example, when her roommate offered to loan her "anything in her closet," Janice wrongly assumed the roommate was insulting her wardrobe (which she felt self-conscious about since she couldn't afford expensive clothing). Thus she responded, "Thanks, but I think I'm smaller than you," which she wasn't. Although she did have three lackluster lovers, she hadn't had a single true relationship or one true friendship.

Building her career was at the top of her life's to-do list. Like everything else, Janice had to work for it. Nothing came easily. She constantly felt that the glass ceiling was preventing her from excelling. She believed she was overlooked for promotions in favor of lesser men. When women were promoted ahead of her, it was because they had slept with the right person or were being controlled by someone – "handled," she would say. What Janice failed to realize was that although she was legitimately quite skilled at her job, she rubbed people the wrong way. The only thing standing in Janice's way was Janice.

As a result of her prickly personality, Janice never became the great success she felt she deserved to be. She had been stuck as an acquisitions editor without hope of becoming publisher. Although she was eventually given the history line to build, she had to fight for each author, each contract, each new idea. And while she found the work more interesting, it was a lateral move. She was merely re-positioned. Despite what she told Prilly, she had been trying to start a memoir line for nearly four years. When Stuart finally agreed, he didn't want her involved with the project at all; he wanted to give it to someone else in-house. Janice had a fit, threatening to sue him for sexual harassment, so he agreed to let her co-edit the line, committing only to a test series. He suggested Prilly because he knew she was able to work well with others, which would balance out the Janice-factor. Janice agreed because after being Prilly's supervisor she had a firm handle on Prilly's weak spots. She also knew that Prilly would never mistakenly see them as partners, as equals.

Janice incessantly boasted to her husband, Richard, that she was much more successful than she truly was. He knew it wasn't true; he saw her paycheck and attended the annual WISE holiday party, where it was very clear that Janice was neither important nor liked. Richard was a highly successful investment banker. He and Janice had met at a bagel store when they were both waiting for a fresh batch of poppy seeds to come out. He was short, only 5'5" (she was two inches taller), and the little hair he had was dark and curly.

Although not terribly attracted to her, he slept with her that night to scratch the itch. *Why not*, he figured. Janice called him twice that week. He was still itchy, so he took her out to Docks Seafood Grill for dinner and then back to his house for a quickie. On their third date, which he thought would probably be their last, they went to a movie and then back to his house where they slept together again. He didn't even get undressed. He just pulled her underwear off from under her dress, pulled his pants down to his ankles, and got on top. He kept his eyes shut so that he could fantasize about his dental hygienist, a fair-skinned redhead who rubbed his arm while the dentist drilled. Janice was fantasizing about one of the college football players she often checked into the fitness center years earlier. He had always smiled at her, revealing his dimples, and he always smelled like cedar.

Richard didn't return any of her calls after that night. Three weeks later, he received a message from her saying that she was a week late getting her period. Once a doctor confirmed that she was pregnant, he asked her to have an abortion. She refused, claiming Catholicism as her reason, though she had long ago deserted the idea of a God, all-loving or otherwise. Richard wasn't the kind of man who wanted to have a child with a woman to whom he wasn't married. This wasn't because he believed in "doing the right thing" as his aging mother urged, but rather because he was embarrassed by it and perceived it as a hassle. After a period of dating, during which they developed a mild friendship, they married at City Hall, with Marge as their only guest, when Janice was seven months pregnant with their only child, a son they named Kyle. He made her sign a prenuptial agreement in exchange for a 2.5-carat, emerald-cut Tiffany diamond. She told everyone that they had eloped in Saint Martin. Janice and Richard hadn't had sex in over four years.

Kyle, now a high school senior, had been Janice's project for years. Desperate to turn him into "something" (he was fairly homely with unwieldy dark hair, a large nose, and oily skin), she schlepped him to museums, sporting events, and ethnic food restaurants. She made him take piano classes (though he had no interest or talent) and karate (though he was terribly uncoordinated). Although Richard was very wealthy with serious family money in addition to a lucrative career, they sent Kyle to public school. This angered Janice but allowed her to tell anyone who would listen all about how important it was that people support the public school system. Always a quiet boy, Kyle had become much more withdrawn in recent years, spending a lot of time alone in his room or out with friends. Janice was initially concerned, but in time, she came to accept it as a normal part of being a teenage boy. She was just glad he had friends. She was too busy to pay much attention. Richard worked twelve-hour days at the office, and then generally spent the remainder of his time, including weekends, locked in his home office, secretly watching televised golf.

Their home was magnificent. Richard bought their split-level brownstone apartment during the big real estate boom in the '90s when the widow of an old cultural attaché finally agreed to sell. It featured high ceilings and mahogany floors and was filled with stunning pieces of antique furniture (many of which were Richard's family heirlooms). Anyone would be jealous of a home like this. Janice truly loved it. She speculated that most of her equally fortunate neighbors barely noticed their own homes. Each day, as she walked through the large, sculpted double doors, she appreciated what she had, often catching herself wandering through the house and looking up, her eyes following the Victorian moldings.

Janice loved being able to say she was married to an investment banker. She loved wearing her diamond ring, which she religiously Windexed once a week for maximum sparkle. She loved showing up at the Christmas party every year with Richard who, at her request, always dressed in an Armani suit. And she loved showing off pictures of Kyle (she always made sure to have blurry pictures, because even she knew what he looked like) who, she bragged, was both musical and athletic. In short, Janice loved the appearance of the life she had pasted together, and tried to suppress the relentless fear that it was all a house of cards.

*

The next few weeks were the most intense of Prilly's life. Every day after work, she hurried to her apartment to freshen up and grab an overnight bag. Then she'd head out to meet Pete at his place or at a teahouse where he often hung out. Some nights they picked up takeout Indian food and ate on Pete's bed, listening to music and talking about art and politics. Other nights they went to underground dance clubs where everyone seemed to know Pete, especially the women. He held her hand as they walked around. It was extraordinary.

She found herself doing things she never thought she would do. The Saturday after they met, they were browsing in a vintage clothing store in the Village when Pete insisted she try on a pair of faux black leather pants. After resisting to no avail, she tried them on. "Well look at you. You're hot, girrrl!" Prilly happily bought them. She wore them four nights later to a club where they danced until three in the morning to wonderful trip-hop music she had never before heard. At his suggestion, Prilly wore silver body glitter on her neck and arms. The next day at work when Janice was in her office babbling on about the potential author list for their series, Prilly had to muster up all of her strength not to blurt out, "I wore body glitter last night. Body glitter! Can you believe it?"

Every night ended the same, with the most intimate lovemaking of Prilly's life. Pete always unflinchingly locked his eyes to hers, except when he entered from behind. She had never felt anything like it. Some nights she took a cab home at four in the morning, others she slept at Pete's. It was always an inner struggle. Although there was nothing that made her happier than falling asleep and waking up with him (sometimes he spooned her and she thought her heart might break from the beauty), she was invariably late to work when she stayed there. Some days she was very late, too late. One day she didn't arrive until almost ten fifteen, which Janice immediately pointed out to her, out of concern of course. Prilly thought tardiness was a small price to pay for the fullness she suddenly felt. She imagined that after another week or so, things would settle down and she would be better able to manage everything.

She knew she was in love with him by the Thursday after they met. As they lay in his bed that morning, he slept soundly as she waited for the alarm clock to beep. He had one of those alarm clocks that begins with four quiet beeps and increases in volume at seven-minute intervals. She was always worried that she wouldn't hear it and often woke herself up shortly before it went off. This, of course, contributed to her increasing exhaustion resulting from her new schedule, a schedule she knew full well couldn't be maintained. He slept for hours after she left, but she had to race to work and then race to meet Pete, who seemed to blossom after ten o'clock. The dark moons under her eyes were becoming more difficult to mask with concealer. On that morning, as she lay awake waiting for the alarm to beep, she kept thinking, *Just a few more minutes, just a few more minutes. Let me lie here with him for just a few more minutes. Don't make it end.* Lying on that old mattress was the most alive she had ever felt. *This is a big life.*

Late one night a week later, lying back to back, Pete whispered, "I love you." It was so quiet she wondered if she had imagined it. She lay awake tightly holding onto the possibility. Two days later, when he said it again, once again as they were falling asleep after making love, she whispered, "I love you, too."

*

Soon Prilly realized that she was working hard to keep Pete's interest. Naturally there was the nearly endless effort to look good: leg shaving, bikini waxes, makeup application, makeup touchups, high heels, and assembling "artsy" outfits that looked effortless. All this dwarfed in comparison to trying to be interesting, which was getting considerably harder. He was always saying clever and insightful things. For example, when they went to the Modigliani exhibit at the MOMA, he explained why the eyes in Modigliani's paintings were so special. She would have missed that. She tried to contribute her own insights about the peculiar shapes of the bodies. Apparently, this was a "pedestrian" remark. Sometimes he was very impressed by her, particularly her quick observations about the use of language (most of which were ideas she had borrowed from her authors). She reveled in the affirmation. Other times he looked at her the way one looks at a dirty puppy that will have to be cleaned. She felt as though there was elixir running through her veins, and she would do anything that she could to keep it flowing. It was a lot of work.

CHAPTER 4

"Hey, Melville, over here," Pete shouted as Melville twice scanned the teahouse. When Melville walked over, he was greeted with, "Fuck man, are you blind?"

Melville sat down at the small table, took off his jacket, and hung it on the back of his chair. "What have you been up to?" Melville asked. "Haven't seen you much lately."

"Aren't you going to order something?"

"No, I don't want anything. If I'm thirsty later I'll just use the water fountain."

"You can't just sit here if you're not going to order anything. You think these people," Pete said as he gestured to the staff behind the espresso bar, "You think these people want you coming in here just to sit?"

Melville didn't say anything. He stood up and got in line. He returned a couple of minutes later with a single shot of espresso. He didn't drink espresso but it was the cheapest thing on the menu and he couldn't afford anything else. When he returned to the table, Pete was reading. He just sat there for a few minutes and then repeated, "What have you been up to? Haven't seen you much lately."

"Been writing. I've nearly got the carnival part just right. And I've been hanging out with that girl, Prilly. Remember the one we met at the Winterson reading?"

Remember? he quipped in his head. He had hardly thought of anything else. "Yeah, she seemed nice."

"Yeah, I like her. She's in publishing, you know. She's been spending most nights at my place. She's meeting me here in about an hour. You can hang and have a coffee with us if you want."

"Sure."

"Clyde's been calling me lately, too. She broke up with that loser and is coming out of her latest bender, so you know. Whatever."

Pete started reading again. Intrigued by this last remark, Melville took a small paperback novel out of his inside jacket pocket and pretended to read.

*

Prilly stared at her watch as she waited in Stuart's office. At first, all she could think about was that she was supposed to meet Pete in twenty minutes. She was going to be late. She tapped her pen against the legal pad on her lap. Soon, she wondered why Stuart had asked to see her before she left. Prilly knew she had been trimming her hours lately and she felt nervous. *I wonder if I look tired. Am I in trouble?* Just as her palms started to sweat, Stuart walked in.

"Sorry to keep you waiting. Marcy cornered me in the mailroom, and you know how hard it is to get away from her."

"No problem. What's up?" Prilly said as a feeling of indigestion bubbled up.

"I wanted to know how it's going with Janice."

"Oh," Prilly said feeling relieved. "It's fine. Everything's going well. She's put a lot of thought into this idea, so I'm really just along for the ride." This wasn't entirely true. While Janice was relentless with emails, voicemails, and unscheduled meetings at her discretion, she also demanded that Prilly implement many of her ideas. In short, she left Prilly to do most of the grunt work. Nevertheless, Prilly didn't want to create any bad blood. Her newfound bliss also made her feel badly for Janice, whom she now saw was so obviously miserable.

"That's good to hear. I bumped into Janice earlier, and she led me to believe that there might have been some friction, division of labor and so forth. I told her I was confident that it could be resolved."

"Oh," Prilly said, stunned. "I'm surprised to hear that."

"I wouldn't give it too much thought. Janice is a bit of a workaholic. I think she holds everyone to her standards. I'm sure it'll be fine."

"I have been working hard Stu. I've just been swamped with everything and this series is taking up a lot of time."

"I know, I know. Don't worry; I just needed to check in. Just wanted to let you know I'm here if needed."

As Prilly stood up and thanked Stu, she remembered that she was late to meet Pete. She had to hurry.

*

Standing at the opposite end of the dining room table from where his mother sat working, Kyle quietly said, "I'm going out now."

"Ok, see you later," Janice softly replied without glancing up from her laptop.

Kyle grabbed his olive green backpack and left, walking two blocks before heading down into the subway. While waiting on the platform, he took his red iPod out of his bag and listened to the Cocteau Twins' *Live BBC Sessions*. A minute later, he was sitting on the train between two elderly women. He got off at the fifth stop and walked with his earphones on up to street level where one of his friends was waiting for him.

"Hey."

"Hey."

*

Prilly, who usually arrived to everything fifteen minutes early, was so late that she skipped her routine stop at home before rushing to the teahouse. She left a toothbrush and some clothes at Pete's place, and had taken to shoving her cosmetic case in her workbag in case of such an emergency. Worried that she might look worn down, she stopped in a Starbucks a block away from the teahouse. After waiting in a long, slow line, she went into the foul-smelling, one-person, unisex bathroom and quickly retouched her makeup. She then raced to meet Pete.

"Hey girl," Pete shouted from a corner table.

Oh great, Melville's here, Prilly thought as she made her way over, trying to slide between cramped tables without knocking her large bag into anything or anyone. She thought that Melville's sunken, drooping eyes made him look like a weirdo, and she also found him oddly quiet. Besides, she was in a bad mood and wanted to be alone with Pete.

"Hey," she said, flopping down on a spare chair and dropping her bag on the floor. "Were you waiting long? I'm really sorry, I got held up at work. You wouldn't believe the crap I'm dealing with."

"All good. No worries. I've been reading a wonderful book," Pete replied.

"I'm beat. Would it be ok if we picked up some takeout and just ate at your place?"

"Yeah, sure," he said as he put his jacket on. He and Prilly left with a quick "See ya later" to Melville.

*

"She's just so two-faced," Prilly said as she maneuvered some lo mein into her mouth.

"Here, let me show you. You're not holding them right," Pete said as he illustrated how to properly place one's fingers on chopsticks.

Embarrassed, Prilly tried to copy him, but moments later resorted back to her own way of holding them.

"Well, is there any truth to it? Have you been pulling your weight?" Pete matter-of-factly asked as he knocked a container of spicy pea pods over onto the old towel that lay across the bed as a makeshift tablecloth.

Unable to control her frustration at what felt like the second betrayal of the day, Prilly snapped back, "She's just a bitch. Don't you get it? I'm doing *most* of the work, not just a little, but most of it. And I never wanted to do this in the first place – she bullied me into it. What the hell is that to say something to my boss when she hasn't said a word to me? She's obviously up to something."

"Well then, you've got to confront her. Take the venom out of it." Before Pete could continue his phone rang. He leaned over and grabbed it off the floor. "Hello?" He turned his back and lowered his voice. "Hey, this isn't a great time. I'm eating with a friend. Where? What's the address? I'll try to make an appearance, but no promises. Yeah. Ok, bye."

Friend??? Prilly thought. *Am I just a friend?* she wondered, as the speed of her animosity built like a runaway car on a rollercoaster straight out of a childhood nightmare.

"Who was that?" she asked most curiously.

"A friend of mine, Clyde. She's having some issues, just broke up with some guy, blah blah blah. She wants to see me. She's going to a small gothic club downtown in a bit. She was hoping I'd make an appearance."

"Oh. Well, I thought we were gonna stay in tonight. I'm tired and upset. I don't really feel like going to a club."

"How about this: why don't you stay here and relax, maybe read or go to sleep, and I'll slip out for a couple of hours?" Pete asked.

Prilly didn't know what to say. *I can't believe that he would leave me here alone. And who is this woman that he wants to see more than he wants to be with me? A woman to whom I am just "a friend?"* She felt like bursting into tears but refused to show him how upset she was, so she coldly said, "Well, I guess, if that's what you want to do, I can just go home."

"No, no, stay here. Stay, relax, listen to music, eat this food, and I'll be back in a couple of hours."

Pete jumped up and walked to the bathroom, bringing the container of lo mein with him. Prilly just sat there. She heard the shower turn on. She heard it turn off. She heard the sink faucet turn on, then off. She heard him open the bathroom door. She mostly heard the angry voice in her head, a high-pitched voice that wouldn't shut up. She just sat there, silently fuming. All she wanted all day was to be with Pete, and now he was ditching her for some other woman. He came into the room and casually said, "Hey girl," and smiled, as if totally unaware of the angst he was causing her. He put the nearly empty Chinese food container down on the bed and said, "That's delicious. I couldn't stop myself," and laughed. As he bent over, she could smell his newly spritzed cologne. She wanted desperately to remain silent, to stay cool. She had been telling herself over and over and over again during his twenty-five minutes in the bathroom that she needed to play it cool. But after that whiff of his cologne, she blurted out, "Who is this friend? Is she an old girlfriend?"

He chuckled. "If you're asking if I've slept with her, yeah, sure, but we're just friends. She's going through a bad time and she wants to talk. I kind of feel like getting out tonight, and you don't. Even if you did, I don't think it would be the best time to introduce you. I broke up with her, and now she just broke up with someone, and you know."

No, I don't know. I don't know why the man I am crazy about, the man I am running all over town to see while utterly exhausted is leaving me to see another woman whom he's slept with, a woman who may still have feelings for him! She could feel rage brewing and feared it would slip from her lips. She held onto it as tightly as she could; worrying that she might induce a stroke.

He leaned down and kissed her on the forehead. As he bent over she heard his black leather pants squeak. They were tight, and with a long black and silver long-sleeved T-shirt over them, he looked sexy. He smelled good, and he looked sexy. She was livid.

*

When Pete left with a "See ya, girl," Prilly experienced physical paralysis and mental Tourette's. She couldn't stop wondering what had just happened. In her mind, over and over again, *What just happened?* Then she started to obsess about Clyde, this woman Pete was so eager to see. She knew he had slept with other women of course, and by his unmatched sexual talents she figured there had been many of them, but she didn't want to think about it; she didn't want to know about them. She mostly didn't want him to care about them. *Clyde, Clyde. She's probably really beautiful. She sounds beautiful. She's probably really cool. She probably wouldn't mind if he ran out to see an old girlfriend. She's probably beautiful.* As she sat in his little apartment that now stunk of Chinese food, a smell she couldn't get rid of long after putting away the leftovers and washing the dishes, she felt sick. The longer she waited, the angrier she got. *Who the fuck is he to leave me like this? What kind of fucking man does this? He doesn't care. He doesn't care about how I feel!*

She decided to get ready for bed and then pretend to sleep until he got home. She wanted to look good, assuming they would make love after he apologized and told her how wonderful she was, so she brushed her teeth but slept with her makeup on. She didn't want to really fall asleep, afraid she would have bad breath and messy hair by the time he returned, so she just lay in bed, thinking, spinning, seething. Four and half hours passed, with each minute experienced like the labored breaths of an old woman on her deathbed. She twice got up to rinse her mouth with Listerine and to powder her nose. She felt pathetic, really pathetic, and she knew she should just get up and leave without a note or phone call, but instead, she lay there counting the seconds. Her thoughts vacillated from Pete to Clyde to Janice and Stuart. Her big life was shrinking.

Shortly after two-thirty, she heard a key in the door. Pete went straight into the bathroom, and ten minutes later, made his way to the bed where Prilly was still pretending to sleep, afraid he could hear her overpowering heartbeats. When he got into bed, she rustled around a bit so he would think he woke her up. He didn't say anything and she could feel his back to her, so eventually she just went to sleep. She woke up at five in a cold sweat, and then fell back asleep.

The next morning Prilly got up, showered and dressed, and made two mugs of coffee with Pete's one-cup coffee maker. There was only a little cream left, and she used most of it in her coffee. *Screw him.* She stood in the kitchen, looking through the cutout wall, trying to read his mind as he slept. *Am I overreacting? Am I being too sensitive? Did it mean anything? Why didn't we make love when he got home?* She couldn't wait for him to wake up and somehow make it better.

After an hour and forty-five minutes of waiting, trying to subtly make just enough noise to wake him without being obvious, he finally woke up, rubbing his eyes and clearing his throat. "Hey. I smell coffee," he said in a low voice.

"Yeah, I made you a cup. You might have to nuke it, it's been sitting for a while."

"K. Thanks," he said as he stood up, wearing the same long-sleeved T-shirt he had left in, now paired with his black boxers. He lifted his arms high into the air and made a loud yawning noise as he stretched upward. "I have to go to the bathroom. I'll be right there."

The next two minutes seemed somehow to be a hundred times longer than all that preceded them. Prilly stood in the kitchen, sipping her cold coffee, not knowing what to do. Pete came in and kissed her on the forehead, grabbed his coffee, and went to the refrigerator for cream. He spilled the last drops into his mug and said, "We're out of cream."

"I know."

He took his mug and walked past her into the bedroom. He propped his pillow against the wall and sat on the bed, legs outstretched, drinking his coffee. Furious, Prilly made a loud sigh and walked into the bedroom with her mug in hand. She sat in the computer chair, and just as Pete started to smile at her, she said, "So, you got home late last night."

"Yeah, sorry. After midnight I figured you were asleep and that it didn't matter, so I stayed a bit longer. Didn't want to call and wake you."

In a sharp tone she responded, "Well, did you have a good time? Is your friend ok?"

"Oh, you know, she's always going through something. She has a tinsel heart, you know. She's like a bird that you want to take care of."

What the fuck is this? Prilly screamed inside her head. *Doesn't he know how upset I am? Can't he see that I'm upset?* The silent anger quickly turned to hurt. *Tinsel heart? Bird? Is everything about her beautiful? It sounds like he loved her. Maybe he still loves her.* Despite all of the thoughts swimming in her mind, she managed to stay silent. It took a lot of effort, but the more special Clyde sounded, the less she wanted to reveal how very not-ok she was with all of this.

"The club was cool. You would like it; we should go sometime. It was very small and dark, and the walls were covered with dark purple fabric, like a flowing translucent kind of fabric. The music was wonderful, a terrific DJ. He played lots of trippy stuff like Portishead. I danced all night."

Fighting every inclination she had, she remained quiet, just looking at him and silently screaming, *What the hell is wrong with you?*

"I'm gonna hop in the shower. Starving. You want to go to that diner again, the one with the fabulous waitress?"

"Sure," she said, feeling relieved that they were spending the day together, but also angry and utterly confused.

Pete got up and went to the bathroom to shower.

*

An hour later, they were sitting in the diner, waiting for someone to take their order. "I'm ravenous; feel like I could eat a horse," Pete said. *He seems particularly jolly this morning*, Prilly thought.

"Hmmm. So you said."

The waitress walked over, and Pete smirked at Prilly; it was not the waitress with the wonderful face. This much younger waitress had a very long, thin face with long, thin features and elfin ears.

She's a bit birdlike, Prilly thought. *Not a pretty bird, but a bird.* She looked at the nametag on her canary-colored uniform: Ruth. *Clyde is probably a beautiful bird*, Prilly imagined.

"I think I'll try an omelet today," Pete said, as if the waitress knew his regular order, or cared. "With mushrooms and cheese, cheddar cheese."

"What kind of toast?"

"Wheat. With marmalade, not jam."

"And for you?"

"Oh, um, I'll have the blueberry pancakes please."

Shit, Prilly thought to herself. *What am I doing? First the lo mein and now pancakes. I'll have to suck in my stomach all day.*

"So what do you want to do today? There's a Shepard Fairey exhibit at the Guggenheim I'm dying to see. Do you know his work?"

"No."

"Oooh, he's wonderful. He's famous for that Obama poster you know, but his other work, his real work, is marvelous. It's all very subversive, like the guerrilla art I told you my friends in London were into. There's a marriage between word and image in the work. Very carefully done. Sharp and sardonic. And the Guggenheim, well fuck, that building is an orgasm itself."

"Uh, huh," Prilly said, totally unable to focus on anything he was saying. She then blurted out, "What happened last night? I mean, you totally ditched me and went out with some woman you've slept with before, and then you don't come home until the middle of the night. Do you know how that makes me feel?" As soon as the words came out, she regretted saying them but was desperate to hear his response.

He laughed. He laughed, and then with a close-mouthed smile, he managed to make her feel even more pathetic than she already felt. "It was nothing. A friend called me and she needed me. You could have come but you weren't up for it. You know how I feel about you. What we have is what we have; it has nothing to do with Clyde or with anyone. It shouldn't matter whether I've slept with her or not."

"Well you might not feel that way if it was you."

"If it were the other way around, I wouldn't care. I know what we have, and I wouldn't worry. I wouldn't want to stop you from doing something you wanted to do."

Unsatisfied, Prilly asked, "Were you … were you in love with her?"

"Love? I don't even know what love is. Love is just a word people say to each other. I care about her, sure."

Love is just a word people say to each other? He doesn't even know what love is? What the fuck is he saying? How can he say this when he told me that he loved me? He said it first, and he said it twice. How can he be saying this? Prilly wondered. What she actually said aloud was, "I felt like you abandoned me. I was really upset; you knew I had a bad day at work, and we made plans. Then you just left. What's worse, you left to see some woman you had a relationship with. How did you think that would make me feel?"

Ruth brought the food over. Pete thanked her and started eating immediately, sprinkling salt on his omelet with one hand as he ate a forkful of home fries with the other. Prilly just sat there, staring at him.

A few moments later, he put his fork down and said, "Look, I'm sorry if you were upset. Honestly, I didn't think it was a big deal. I thought you were cool with it."

"Ok, I guess we can just drop it," Prilly responded, not quite sure if she had blown it all into something bigger than it was, but certain she didn't want things to escalate further. She cut up her pancakes, drizzled on some syrup, and ate, trying to convince herself she wasn't really as upset as she was.

After a few bites Pete said, "You know, I don't believe in the traditional monogamy thing. I mean, I thought we were cool, that we had an unspoken understanding, but maybe it's best to lay our cards on the table." Unable to take in the oxygen necessary to comprehend this information or formulate a response, Prilly sat silently. Pete continued, "I mean, we're having a wonderful time and it's very special, so there's no reason to label it. What a person has with one person doesn't diminish what they have with someone else. Like with Clyde. What I had with her doesn't take away from how I feel about you. It's totally different."

Too many thoughts, too many thoughts to process, Prilly frantically thought to herself. She took another bite of blueberry pancake in order to buy enough time to steady her voice. "I don't understand. We've spent every day together since we met." Leaning in and lowering her voice, she said, "You told me you loved me."

He again smiled, close-mouthed. "I said what was in my heart in the moment. I always do and it is always true. This you can count on. So who needs false promises when you have that?"

She thought to herself that maybe this Clyde woman, whoever she was (and she did sound wonderful), could see the beauty in what Pete was saying; she probably could, "tinsel heart" and all, but to Prilly, it just felt hurtful, deeply hurtful. She wondered if they had been in the same relationship at all. She felt foolish.

"I still don't understand. Are you saying that you're seeing other people or that you want to? Did something happen with Clyde last night? Is that why you came back so late?"

He offered up another close-mouthed smile. "No, no, nothing happened with Clyde if that's what this is really about, but even if it had, it wouldn't need to change anything we have. Clyde was once a special person in my life, and she is still sort of in my life, but I haven't slept with her since we broke up before I met you. I think she wanted to last night. She was very vulnerable. But truthfully, all I could think about was you at my place, in my bed, waiting for me. I thought it was sweet how you let me go, how you knew it was ok."

Again, too many thoughts; too many thoughts to process at once, Prilly thought, feeling overloaded. He had thrown so much information at her, and she feared none of it was good. She wanted to be cool. She wanted to be the sweet, cool, tinsel-hearted girl who waited in his bed. But she wasn't. So, she responded sharply, "It would matter to me."

"Look, two people can be together forever and be only with each other, but not because of some artificial promise. I don't believe in that. Sure, you can find a thousand men with who will give you hollow promises, but that's not me. That's not what I'm giving you. You have to live moment to moment, and the moments string together. And eventually you can string together a lifetime, but not because of promises, just because it is true to your heart, to your soul. You cannot cage a bird, as they say."

Great, more birds, Prilly thought. "It wouldn't be all right with me if you were with someone else. That's not what I want."

He smiled again, letting out the quietest of laughs as if she were too provincial to understand what he was saying or too insecure to deal with it, the latter of which may well have been true.

"Ok, I understand. If anything were to ever happen with someone else, or if I wanted it to, I would tell you. You have my word. I would be honest with you and you could do as you needed to."

"Ok," Prilly softly said, not knowing how to make this dreadful conversation end in a way that would leave them both sitting there, and ideally in a way that would restore the feeling to her numb feet.

"But I don't want to be with anyone else right now. I like being with you," he said, as if he were giving her a gift. Just as she had so many times in earlier years, she felt like Charlie Brown dumping out a Christmas stocking full of coal.

*

On the way to the Guggenheim, Pete wanted to "dash into Starbucks for a doppio espresso." He said he was still feeling "wiped and the diner coffee sucked." When he and Prilly hurried in, she noticed Melville sitting by the window. This time, she was glad to see him. "I'll just have a bottle of water please," she said to Pete as she plopped down next to Melville. Pete put his hand out. Embarrassed on every level, Prilly reached into her bag scrambling for her wallet. She pulled out a five and handed it to him. "Do you want anything?" she asked Melville. Not accustomed to being offered anything, he just shook his head. "So, what's up?" she asked.

"Um, nothing really. Just reading a book," Melville shyly replied.

Prilly grabbed the book from him. "Wow, this looks good. I love novels set in Victorian times." She glanced over to spot Pete whooping it up with the pretty, young barista behind the counter. Suddenly, she was replaying their relationship in her head. She thought these had been the best weeks of her life, but now, as she rewound, all she could picture were the times he flirted with waitresses, made small talk with female bartenders, or spoke to strange women in cafés after she had hurried from work to meet him. Feeling terribly insecure and in need of affirmation she looked at Melville, who she had an inkling might like her, and said, "You know, Melville, I met you when I met Pete. Remember? Did you ever think it might be different? That it could have been different that day, and you and I might have ended up together?"

With a stone face concealing his astonishment, he stuttered a bit and said, "Well, you and Pete seem to make a good couple." Secretly, he thought, *Yes, yes, I think about it all the time, and I hate myself for not having been able to talk to you first, knowing it never would have been me.*

Totally distracted by his last "couple" comment, she was markedly unaware of the effect she was having on Melville, who felt increasingly tortured. She slumped down, balancing her elbows on the table and putting her head in her hands, and muttered, "Yeah, well, couple. What's a couple, right?"

Melville was too caught up in his own thoughts to realize how incoherent she was. Like most people, Prilly was speaking to a tape in her head that no one else could hear. "Hey Melville, do you know Clyde?"

"Yeah, sure."

Prilly leaned in closer, "She and Pete were a thing, right?"

"Yeah, I thought they were the real thing."

As Melville's heart raced at the smell of Prilly's apple-blossom shampoo, Prilly's heart sank at the confirmation of her worst fear: Pete had been in love with Clyde.

Suddenly, Prilly heard Pete say, "Thanks, hon" to the barista in his ever-sexy voice. She leaned back, feeling defeated. When Pete returned, he handed Prilly the bottled water – without change, she noticed – and remarked, "You know the plastic in these things is probably worse than the tap water. Ha. All these supposedly environmentally conscious people drink these, but what do they think all of these plastic bottles do to the environment? That's an inconvenient truth," Pete said through intermittent laughter.

Prilly was in no mood to be criticized. She was heartbroken and he was lecturing her about her beverage choice.

"Ready to go?" he asked.

Oblivious as ever, Prilly thought. "Sure. Why doesn't Melville come along?" Prilly suggested, surprising them both.

After a brief pause Melville said, "Oh, no it's ok."

"No, come on. We're going to the Guggenheim to see some art exhibit Pete's all excited about. Come with us. It'll be fun."

"Come with us, don't just sit here all day," Pete said. Somehow even his invitation made Melville appear feeble.

"Ok."

And with that, the three made their way on foot to the Guggenheim.

CHAPTER 5

Janice had a very particular weekend routine. Every Saturday she woke up bright and early and hurried out of bed with great urgency only to discover her family was nowhere to be found. Her husband was already out. She invariably assumed that he must be at the squash club, which was his weekend morning ritual. Kyle was either sleeping or out; she assumed he left early in the morning, but never quite knew for sure if he had ever returned the night before. It never occurred to her that surely they would be gone, so she always went through the ritual of searching for them before concluding they were out.

Then she raced to the kitchen in her long, tangerine kimono purchased when "Asian styles" were in, and made a pot of decaffeinated coffee. She always bought whatever brand was on sale, normally some sort of dry-roasted Colombian blend in a large canister covered with dust. She emptied the dishwasher as the coffee dripped. Then she filled her Cornell College mug, adding only one Splenda, and trotted off to her bedroom to make the bed, complete with military corners. She then went to her makeshift office in the dining room, checked her email, and read her favorite blog, a humorous pop-feminist blog by a Canadian writer from whom she stole many ideas. Next, she decided to "do a little work." She typically worked for several hours, getting up occasionally to refill her coffee or grab a bunch of grapes. She rarely had work that required her to work these extended hours, so she simply obsessed about the work that she did have, often coming up with piles of "new ideas" that Stu later rejected. She also enjoyed creating lists of "things to do" for her various projects, followed by lists of what could be outsourced (mostly to Prilly).

By late morning, she needed to "clear her head," which she accomplished by riding her stationary bicycle in the windowless guest room across from her second-floor bedroom. Sometimes she watched public television on the small, old TV in the room. After exercising she showered and got ready for the day. Next, lunch.

Typically this consisted of a sandwich of some kind, which she ate at the dining room table and usually decided to "do a little more work while she's sitting there." By late afternoon, Kyle made an appearance. Although he often stopped by the dining room to chat with her, by then she was always deeply engrossed in her unnecessary work. She wouldn't look up, so Kyle would leave. By five thirty, with the day gone and no longer able to stare at her computer screen, she wandered around her house until it was time to go out with her husband. They usually had a work-related dinner with his colleagues. She did her best to make conversation but found it tiresome. She often complained to Richard's colleagues that she was so overloaded with work. She'd say, "I had to work all day, yet again. Can you believe it? I can't remember the last time I I had a day off." Sensing his colleagues felt badly for her, she felt free to talk more about the demands of publishing "at her level." She always thought these dinners went very well considering how stressed she was. On nights when there was no business obligation, they sometimes went out to dinner alone, making small talk about getting the car checked or taking Kyle to the dentist. Other nights Janice just spent the evening by herself, eating takeout in bed and watching television. Sundays were almost exactly the same except she called her sister and they never went out to dinner.

By the time she got to work on Monday, she was angry that she had been so swamped with work that she hadn't been able to enjoy her weekend. She was especially difficult to deal with, particularly to those who made the mistake of telling her about how they had spent their weekend.

There were only two exceptions to her weekend routine. First, Janice and Richard took a vacation twice a year. Every spring they spent one week in Phoenix visiting Richard's sister, Vicki, and brother-in-law, James. Janice and Vicki usually spent afternoons together going to local craft markets. Janice always bought some silver and turquoise jewelry crafted by Native Americans. She haggled over the price well past the point of acceptability by anyone else's standards. Vicki was mortified but never said anything, since it was the only time all year she "had" to see Janice. Over lunch, Janice would go on and on about how she liked to "buy the local crafts to support the Native Americans." Desperate for an anesthetic, Vicki usually ordered a glass of white wine with her lunch and said that it was a "special occasion, a girl's day."

Richard and James spent mornings at a local health club. James hated playing squash with Richard; Richard took it far too seriously and had James running around the court the whole time. When they returned to the house, Richard excused himself to work. Not only did he bring his laptop, Blackberry, and Bluetooth headset, but he scheduled lengthy conference calls. Late in the afternoon Vicki would say she was a bit tired from the wine at lunch and would excuse herself for a nap. She usually lay on her bed watching the Travel Channel on mute. Janice sat outside on their wrap-around porch admiring the exquisite scenery. The dramatic landscape composed of shades of burnt umber impressed her. Before marrying Richard, she had never seen anything like it. After half an hour on the porch she invariably wound up at their dining room table with her laptop, working.

In the evenings, they all went out to dinner. When Kyle and his cousin Natashya were younger, they were there too – requiring parental attention so that there was little need for the adults to come up with conversation. Since Natashya went to college to study film at NYU two years earlier, Kyle refused to go on the trips. This allowed them to talk about their kids when they had exhausted their supply of small talk about "how wonderful dinner is" and "how great it is to take some time off for family." Vicki secretly harbored anger toward Janice and Richard for not extending themselves more to Natashya while she was living in New York. They had invited her over for dinner only once (Chinese takeout) and taken her to one Broadway show (*Wicked*) in the two years she had lived in the city. James didn't know why Vicki found that so offensive.

On their other annual trip, Janice and Richard visited an exotic Caribbean island for a week. They stayed at a five-star resort. Janice loved being waited on by the staff. When they stayed at the Four Seasons in Nevis, the cabana boys walked around on the beach spraying guests with Evian water. Janice couldn't get enough of it, although she also felt that she had snuck into a member's only club and might be caught at any moment. To compensate for her insecurity, she was overly demanding of the staff, to make sure they knew she belonged there. This was the only time all year when Janice and Richard really spent time together. Mostly they lounged on the beach, each reading their own book. Richard often worked on his laptop in the evenings after dinner, and Janice went to sleep alone. When she returned from these trips she boasted about her fabulous vacation for weeks to anyone in the office she could corner long enough to listen.

The other exception to her weekend routine was when she met one of her girlfriends for lunch, sometimes followed by shopping or a museum visit. She only had three friends with whom she spent time by herself, and although she enjoyed an occasional lunch, during which they caught up on work, kids, and so forth, she never created any real intimacy. The conversation, at least on her end, was always superficial. She liked having friends who would share their problems with her, and to whom she could complain about how hard she was forced to work and how undervalued she was. These conversations made her feel good about herself.

On this particular Saturday, she had lunch plans with her friend, Sarah Cohen, a feminist historian she met at a WISE event years ago. As usual, she woke up with the sun that morning to discover Richard was already out. *He's probably playing squash at the club*, she thought to herself. After making her decaf coffee and checking her email, she decided to jump on the exercise bike for an hour and then get ready to meet Sarah. She chose her favorite charcoal gray pencil skirt paired with a thin, black V-neck sweater. While she dressed, she started to regret making plans with Sarah. She wasn't in the mood to hear about her boyfriend, a public school teacher whom Janice had met once at a book party. Sarah had a way of being particularly draining. As she unrolled her black tights up one leg at a time, she thought about how Sarah would go on and on, and Janice wished she could stay at home to get some work done.

Janice arrived everywhere early. When she went out on weekends, she carried the streamlined black Prada pocketbook Richard had given her for Christmas two years earlier (he always gave her a "statement piece" on Christmas, her birthday, and their anniversary, and she adored them). She was able to slide one manila folder of work into the thin rectangular bag. She felt less self-conscious waiting for someone if she had a project to occupy her. It also sent a powerful message to the person who, in Janice's mind, was late and wasting her time. (To Janice, "late" was anything after she arrived, though she routinely arrived fifteen minutes early, making it nearly impossible for any normal person not to be "late.")

Despite trying to feign interest in the folder of memoir series notes, Janice noticed Sarah immediately when she arrived at the restaurant at noon (Janice naturally clocked her in at fifteen minutes late). It was hard not to notice Sarah. An ex-hippy, she wore long, flowing, Indian-inspired, multi-colored skirts with tank tops adorned with many long layers of ornate chains or large beads. On this day, Sarah was wearing a long, merlot-colored skirt with a black pattern of some indiscernible kind, a white tank top, and four multi-length necklaces of silver coins that sounded like wind chimes every time she moved. Sarah was petite and very pretty, with waist length, nearly black hair in natural spiral curls. Janice thought Sarah would be beautiful if she dressed in more sophisticated clothing and tamed her hair. Paradoxically, she admired her for having her own unique style. Janice always experienced some dread before seeing Sarah, but when they were together, she remembered the many things she liked about her. On this day, the always-effervescent Sarah couldn't stop talking.

"Oh, there's my friend," Sarah hollered as she floated past the hostess, who pointed to the far corner where Janice had taken the booth seat. "Hi, hi, hi. Oh, don't get up," she said as she slid into the chair across from Janice, throwing her large canvas tote on the chair beside her. "Hope I didn't keep you waiting. I'm starving."

"Oh, no, it's fine. I was just catching up on some work."

"Busy?" Sarah asked as she read the menu.

Janice sighed and gently moved a strand of hair that was aggravating her eye. "I'm swamped. I'm telling you, you can't even imagine."

"I hope they appreciate you over there."

"Ha. You can't imagine. It's a real mess there. I work more than anyone and they don't like it. They're threatened by me. I'm a big producer, and it makes others look bad, so they try to marginalize me as much as they can. No one's doing me any favors, that's for sure. If I wasn't committed to my authors, I'll tell you, I wouldn't bother."

"That's awful. There's so much of a bias against women, too. I bet if you were a man they'd be in awe of you, but because you're a woman they're threatened."

"Absolutely," Janice said as she nodded while thinking to herself that sometimes Sarah was really spot-on.

"Well, have I got a story for you. It'll take your mind off of work," Sarah said as the waiter came over and asked if they wanted to order a drink.

"Actually, I think we're ready to order lunch," Janice responded. Sarah nodded as she scoured the menu. "I'll have a club soda with lime and the chicken tortilla salad," Janice said.

"And for you, Miss?" the waiter asked, unable to stop staring at Sarah.

"An iced tea, unsweetened, and the beet salad without cheese. Thanks."

"Very good."

"I stopped eating dairy a month ago, and I feel terrific," Sarah told Janice, as if to explain her order.

"What do they call that? Vegan?" Janice asked.

"Yeah, now I'm a full-fledged vegan. I read an op-ed in *The New York Times* that reported reducing meat intake by twenty percent is the equivalent of going from driving a Toyota Camry to driving a Prius. Can you believe it? So I figured since I didn't miss meat when I gave that up I would try the non-dairy thing too. It's been terrific. I'm full of energy."

"Uh huh," Janice said, suddenly thinking Sarah sounded stupid.

"So, you're not going to believe this. Remember that Israeli-Palestinian peace group I'm in?"

"Uh huh," Janice said, even though she didn't. Sarah was always hung up on some new cause or joining some new group, none of which interested Janice so she didn't keep track.

"Well, we lined up a panel of speakers to coincide with the New York City Human Rights Festival. Remember I forwarded you that email?"

Janice nodded.

"Anyway, I somehow volunteered for the party planning committee for the opening reception. Just a low-key social event, wine and appetizers kind of thing. We had, like, no budget, so there's only so much you can do. Someone suggested doing the food potluck style, which I thought was a great idea. Save money, get the people on the committee involved, easy for me."

"Uh huh," Janice said, looking intently at Sarah despite being already bored with the story.

"Well, days before the reception I get a call from Joanne, who is also on the planning committee and is kind of the main de facto organizer of our group. Apparently, a couple of kosher people who aren't members of our group wanted to come to the event, but requested that only kosher food be served. Joanne told them that wasn't going to be possible since arrangements had already been made, but that they were welcome to contribute kosher dishes to the buffet."

"Uh huh. Did that satisfy them?" Janice asked, trying to show that she was paying attention.

"Nope. Not at all. They said that it would not be acceptable to serve non-kosher food at this kind of event. I'll spare you every detail, but suffice it to say, Joanne wanted to get this person off the phone so she told him to call me. I talked to the guy and got a long education about what it means to prepare and serve a kosher buffet and that simply adding a kosher-made dish would not suffice. I told him we did not intend to serve shrimp wrapped in bacon, but that we had some Palestinian committee members who were planning on serving hummus and salads. I thought that maybe dishes that didn't contain meat might be ok."

"And?" Janice asked, totally missing Sarah's humor regarding the bacon-wrapped shrimp.

"He said that he understood but wouldn't be able to attend. So after a year and a half of volunteering with this peace process group,

I couldn't even get people to agree on a politically and culturally acceptable buffet! How do you like that?"

Janice smiled. "Religion is a tough thing to battle. People are very sensitive about it," she said in a serious tone that was incongruous with Sarah's zealous storytelling.

"Doesn't give me much hope for world peace," Sarah said, now unable to control her laughter. The waiter returned with their salads and they ate lunch.

Sarah was meeting her boyfriend that afternoon to see a series of documentary shorts at a nearby independent movie theater. She invited Janice, who insisted she needed to get some more work done. They hugged at the door of the restaurant and parted ways. It was such a beautiful, crisp day that Janice decided to walk home. On the way, she stopped at a corner grocer. She looked at the flowers extensively but hated spending money on something so fleeting. She ended up picking up some pink lady apples and a bottle of cranberry juice and headed home.

*

That night, Melville approached his apartment with dread. He could hear hip-hop music blaring from the downstairs corridor and knew Jacob was probably having another awful party. When he opened the apartment door, a wave of smoke assaulted him. He coughed as he made his way through the small, darkened living room lined wall-to-wall with people he had never seen. No one seemed to notice him as he went straight to his room. He flung his jacket on his chair, staring longingly at the Mozart CD case on his desk. He lay on his couch with his hands behind his head. He thought he could see his room vibrating with each blast of reverberated noise. Eventually, he shut his eyes. He wanted to masturbate but was scared someone would walk in so he pulled his blanket up to his chest, unzipped his pants, and did it quickly.

*

As they arrived back at Pete's apartment, Prilly felt increasingly anxious. All she could think about was Pete leaving the night before, Clyde (a stranger whom she suddenly couldn't stop wondering about), and worst of all, those awful words at the diner: *love is just a word ... I don't even know what love is ... I don't believe in promises ... I will tell you if I want to be with someone else.* Over and over she replayed his words and Melville's remark that Pete and Clyde were the "real thing." Her brain was a muddled mess interspersed with images of Pete intently looking at her while they made love and how she felt so alive she could see sounds and hear colors.

She mindlessly followed Pete into the apartment. He was still talking about the Fairey exhibit.

"The consumerism stuff is a bit pedestrian but good anyway. I mean, I've seen more inventive stuff. The whole church-state thing has been done. But you gotta hand it to him, the collection as a whole makes a statement."

"Uh huh."

"There was some filler, though. The portraits of the musicians are fun but disconnected from the larger work. I mean, yeah, they're all resistive counter-culture artists, but they're not political in the ways he's suggesting. I mean, I get the subversive artist thing, but it didn't all hang together like the other work. I would have done it differently."

"Uh huh. Yeah, I liked those pieces though. Music gets at people in its own way," Prilly said as she plopped down on the edge of the bed, tossing her bag on the ground.

"Hey you," Pete said in his sexiest voice as he glanced over through the cutout wall from the kitchen where he was guzzling a canned energy drink.

She smiled at him.

As he made his way over to her, she couldn't quiet her mind. *What's going on? What is this? What am I doing here? How does he feel about me? Why does he look at me that way if he doesn't love me? Why? How could he want to be with someone else when I can only think of him?*

With one touch of his hand to her shoulder, her thoughts scampered and she looked up at him, hoping for a sign. As they made love, her eyes locked onto him. She kept thinking, *He will see what I am trying to show him. He will see what I feel and he will tell me he feels the same. I know he does.*

Afterward, she lay in his arms waiting, making a conscious effort not to fall asleep. If he held her long enough, after that beautiful, intimate lovemaking, he would give his whole self to her, as she thought he once did.

"You're beautiful."

She smiled softly as she looked up into his eyes.

"Are you hungry? I'm starving. I think I have some pasta. I could make a little spicy tomato sauce. I think I have some olives and capers. Want to help?" he asked as he sat up and grabbed his boxers from the floor.

"Sure, that sounds good," she said as she sat up. Prilly got dressed as Pete headed to the kitchen.

They fell asleep two hours later after a pasta and red wine dinner eaten in bed followed by Pete reading more pages from his latest work. Prilly thought she was happy, but that night she woke up three times in a cold sweat. The last time she awoke, Pete was holding her as he slept.

When she woke up in the morning, she was surprised to find Pete already out of bed. "Hey girrrl. You're a sleepyhead. I made you some coffee."

"What time is it?" she asked, rubbing the corners of her eyes.
"It's only ten thirty. I woke up feeling inspired this morning and had to get some stuff down. Funny how the brain works. That stuff we saw yesterday gave me some new ideas."

"That's great," Prilly said as she sat up and reached over the side of the bed in search of her underwear.

"I've been onto the word-image thing for years. I mean, that's the whole graphic novel game when it's done right, but the way Fairey has whittled it down to literally marry the singular word and image, it's clever."

"Uh huh," Prilly said as she realized she was putting her tank top on backwards. Pete was still talking as she went to the bathroom to brush her teeth. She usually got up first expressly so she could freshen up before he awoke. When she came out, he said, "Come see this," and motioned over to her from in front of his computer.

"Sure, let me grab my coffee," she said sleepily.

With her coffee in hand, she walked over and stood next to Pete, who put his right arm around her and pointed to the screen with his left. She scanned the words in front of her while sipping her coffee. "I like it. It's ironic, right?"

"Yeah. It's supposed to be humorous. But notice how I do that without diminishing the message."

"Yeah, it's good. I ..." but before Prilly could continue, the phone rang.

Pete jumped up and pushed past her. "Hang on, babe. Hold that thought." Prilly sat down in front of the computer and started scrolling down. "Hey, it's not a good time. Yeah, sure. Will do. Bye." He hung up the phone and returned to the computer. "So girl, tell me what you think."

"Who was that?"

"Clyde," he nonchalantly replied.

"Oh."

"I told her I'd call her back," he said as he kissed the top of Prilly's head. "I know how it bothers you, so I can wait and talk to her later after you've left."

"So basically you're saying that you'll just talk to her behind my back?" Prilly shouted as she leapt up, knocking Pete back.

"What the hell?"

As Prilly hurried across the room and knelt to the floor where her clothes lay strewn, she continued her tirade, "You just don't get it. You don't understand how I feel. You don't care." She frantically picked up her things and jammed them into her overnight bag.

"What are you talking about?" Pete said, now sounding annoyed. "Of course I care about your feelings. That's why I didn't talk to her now. I wanted to avoid this melodrama. It's not behind your back. I haven't lied to you," his voice rapidly elevating.

Putting her shoes on as quickly as possible, she shouted, "You don't get it. You don't fucking get it," and she jumped up with her bag in hand.

"Fuck you. I don't need this shit. I haven't done anything wrong. You're crazy," Pete hollered.

Prilly stormed out, slamming the door so loudly Pete was afraid it would come unhinged like she had.

*

Prilly opened the door to her apartment with her shoulders slumped, feeling physically unable to take another step. On the way home, her rage had given way to a heaviness that she had never felt before. She dropped her bag by the door and went straight into her bedroom. She took off her shoes, got into bed, and pulled the covers over her head. She shut her eyes and begged God to let her fall asleep. When she woke up a couple of hours later, she started crying and couldn't stop. After several hours of uninterrupted sobbing, she got up, put her robe on over her clothes, and went to the kitchen. She opened a bottle of wine while an emergency frozen fish sticks dinner cooked in the microwave. Feet dragging, she brought her meal into the living room where she nibbled and watched two Lifetime movies starring Valerie Bertinelli. The second movie was based on the true story of a mentally ill woman who stormed an elementary school with a gun and randomly shot a child in a brutal conclusion. In an earlier scene that Prilly would never forget, the increasingly fragile woman compulsively bought raw meat at the grocery store and filled her otherwise empty refrigerator with it – the meat eventually started to spill out into her apartment. It was insane. Prilly wondered why the woman did that. Did it make her feel better? Then she imagined the feeling of her hand penetrating a lump of ground meat.

*

Janice's phone rang at two thirty in the afternoon. The ringing was a jarring interruption to the usual stillness. She got up from her dining room table where she was checking her email and walked into the kitchen to answer the phone. "Hello?"

"Hey sis, it's me."

Surprised because they had already had their weekly call several hours earlier, Janice stumbled a bit before saying, "Oh, hi. What's up? Did you forget something?"

"Something happened. Something bad."

Janice leaned against the wall and lowered her voice. "What is it, Marge? What happened?"

"Dad was hit by a car. It's bad."

Janice stood against the wall, breathing slowly and trying to process what Marge had said. "How bad? Where is he?" she asked.

"He's at Mercy. He's in critical condition, Jan. We don't know if he'll make it. They don't know the extent of his injuries yet. His legs were mangled. If he survives, he may not ever be able to walk again. Mom is hysterical. Scott is watching the boys while I wait with her. Depending on how things go, he and I will take turns staying here with Mom."

"Well that's good. That's good," Janice mumbled. Calmly, she asked, "How did this happen?"

"The guy who hit him said he was just walking across the freeway. It was a college kid, Jan. We're told he's devastated. I feel so sorry for him. I mean, who would expect an elderly man to be walking across the freeway? I mean, not a street but the middle of the damn freeway!"

"What freeway? Why was Pop walking across the freeway?"

"Mom said he was going to sit by the lake. It's a beautiful day, which we don't get many of this time of year. She said he likes to watch the birds. There's a pedestrian overpass for people to cross the freeway safely, but Mom said he always complained that it was too long. I guess he decided to take a shortcut and cross the freeway instead. Crazy. I mean, who would cross a damn freeway on foot? Scott and I feel really sorry for the kid who hit him."

"That's awful."

Without hesitation Marge continued, "It's probably his drinking spot, Jan. I mean, watch the birds? Give me a break. I never thought of Dad as a nature lover." Marge took a long pause before saying, "I don't have the heart to say anything to Mom. She believes his bullshit. Jan, he was probably drunk and didn't know what he was doing. That's the only explanation I can think of."

"If he was drunk, the doctors would have said something. They test people for that stuff, Marge. We don't know what happened yet. Let's wait and see."

Marge sighed, knowing she and Janice would never see their father the same way – or their mother, whom Marge became fairly close to once she was old enough to take pity on her. They had long ago agreed not to talk about their parents. "I think you should come home. I think you should get on the first flight you can. Ask Richard to come with you."

Flustered, Janice swiftly responded, "I can't. I'm inundated at work. I can't just pick up and leave right now. I have too many responsibilities, too many commitments. What good would my presence do? There's nothing I can do. Richard can't do anything, and he couldn't leave work even if he wanted to. Richard doesn't even know Dad. And you don't even know what's what at this point."

After a long pause, during which Marge clearly tried to collect her thoughts, she said, "Mom could use the support, Jan."

"I'll call her. I will. I'll call her as soon as you let me know she's back in the house. If things get worse, I'll come but I can't drop everything now. I have no choice. Try to understand."

Not surprised, Marge replied, "I'll call you later and let you know what's going on. Please think about coming. I could use you here too, Jan."

"Ok. Keep me posted. Take care of yourself," Janice whispered.

"Will do. Bye."

"Bye."

As Janice hung up the phone, she felt a bit dizzy so she stood for a few moments, just balancing, trying to reclaim her equilibrium. Then she walked back into the dining room, sat down in front of her computer, opened her memoir notes, and began working.

At five thirty, Kyle came home. "Hey Mom," he shouted as he walked upstairs to his room.

"Hi," she said, still mesmerized by her computer screen.

Half an hour later Richard came home. He had something big going on at work and spent most of the day in his office. He walked past her on his way to the kitchen.

"Should we order Chinese?" he asked as he twisted the cap off a small bottle of Vitaminwater.

"Sure, that's fine. I'll have my usual."

"Is Kyle here?"

"Yes, he's in his room," she said without diverting her eyes from her computer.

"Kyle? Kyyyle," Richard shouted.

"Yeah, Dad?" he replied from the top of the stairs.

"We're ordering Chinese. What do you want?"

"Beef and broccoli, and some of those ravioli – the fried ones. Thanks."

"Ok."

Richard picked up the phone, hit 3 on their speed dial, and placed their order.

An hour later, they quietly ate dinner together, all seated at one end of the table as Janice's folders occupied the other. They used paper plates. After dinner, Kyle went to his room for the rest of the evening while Richard watched a football game in the living room and Janice watched a PBS special on Irish stepdancing in bed. At eleven thirty, Richard came up to their room. Without speaking, they carried out their nightly routine of taking turns at the bathroom sink to brush their teeth. When Richard switched out the lights and got into bed, Janice said, "My father was in an accident today. He was hit by a car."

"That's terrible," Richard said loudly, turning to her.

Lying on her back and staring at the ceiling, Janice replied, "Yeah, Marge is really upset. It's bad."

"Is he going to be ok?"

"Don't know."

"How did it happen?"

"I don't know. He was just crossing the street," she softly said. She turned onto her side, away from Richard, and said, "Goodnight."

He lay looking at her back for a moment and then said, "Goodnight." He rolled over and they fell asleep back-to-back.

The next morning Janice was in her office at eight fifteen.

*

Prilly called in sick for only the second time since starting at WISE (the first time she had eaten some bad sushi for dinner, which caused her to wake up at three in the morning and left her unable to get off the toilet until the next afternoon). She spent the day lying on her couch, curled up under a pink chenille blanket, watching talk shows and court TV. She kept thinking Pete would call to apologize, but he didn't. As the hours rolled on, she thought about the things he said to her. *Maybe I was being irrational. He's allowed to have friends.* By that evening, Prilly was sure that she had blown it. She overreacted. She wanted to call to tell him but felt frozen. She didn't know what to say, and she was embarrassed. By late evening, her thoughts drifted from Pete to work. She wondered how she would be able to go to the office the next day. She felt like crap. She wasn't ready to face the world. She decided to set her alarm for the usual time and take it from there. When the alarm went off the next morning at six, she felt too depressed to get out of bed. She called in sick again and watched a *People's Court* marathon on TV while napping intermittently on her couch.

When she arrived at work at nine fifteen on Wednesday morning, Janice immediately cornered her in her office, walking right into the open door without knocking or saying a word.

"Oh, hi Janice. How are you?"

"Is everything all right, Prilly?" Janice asked in a demanding voice as she made herself at home.

"Yeah, everything's fine …"

Before she could continue, Janice sternly asked, "Well where have you been? I've been swamped here, neck deep in our series and you've been nowhere to be found."

"I was home sick. I had the flu. I called in."

"Well, you should have called or emailed me too, Prilly. I mean, we're working together now and I need to be able to count on you. Authors are emailing me queries, agents are sending me proposals, and you're nowhere to be found. I've been on my own dealing with all of this and with all of my other responsibilities. I've emailed you several times."

Prilly had no idea why Janice seemed so angry; it wasn't as if she had missed any deadlines or scheduled meetings. "I haven't checked my email yet. Sorry if you've been stuck because I was out. I was really sick and there's no way I could have come in. I never miss work; you know that. Anyway, I'm sorry."

"Uh huh," Janice replied in a sharp tone while nodding. She then stood up and said, "Please deal with the emails I forwarded to you."

"Ok," Prilly said as Janice walked to the door.

Right before Janice left, she turned to face Prilly and said, "I'm just looking out for you, Prilly. People were talking, wondering where you were. I don't want to see you under the gun." She walked out in a huff, leaving Prilly to wonder why she had ever agreed to work with Janice and whether people had really been talking.

Prilly spent the rest of the week trying to concentrate on work. She stayed in the office until after eight thirty each night. Janice thought Prilly was trying to show that she was on top of things. Really, Prilly was wasting so much time during the day because she was unable to focus – time spent daydreaming about Pete and berating herself – that she needed the extra time in order to get a bare minimum of work done. She also couldn't stand to be alone in her apartment, waiting for the phone to ring. Even though just a month earlier, spending time alone in her apartment would have been fine, everything was different now. She wished she were with Pete every moment she was alone there. In those long solitary moments, she grew to blame herself even more. She had tasted happiness and spit it out, too afraid to swallow.

Saturday morning she slept until eleven. She didn't bother to shower since she had nowhere to go. Wearing the robe that had recently become her at-home uniform, she drank her coffee and decided to do something drastic. She would just show up at the teahouse Pete frequented, and maybe she could accidentally bump into him. She knew it was pathetic and she hated herself a little for wanting to do it, but after two hours spent getting ready (making sure her hair was shiny and her outfit was artsy-sexy-casual), she found herself approaching the teahouse.

Her heart was racing and her palms were sweaty. She feared passing out. *This might be a mistake. This might be a really big mistake.* These fears echoed in her head as her hand reached for the door, now so sweaty that she left a perspiration handprint on the gold knob as she walked in. She tried to appear casual, but she hurried to the counter so fast that she wasn't able to scan the whole room to see if he was there. When it was her turn in line, she stuttered. "Uh, uh, I'll have a … a latte, non-fat. Uh, small please."

As she waited for her beverage, she noticed Melville sitting in the corner by the front window. He was writing in a spiral notebook and didn't seem to notice her. As she went to the condiment counter to get a napkin, she discretely scoured the place only to discover that Pete wasn't there. She felt stupid. She decided to talk to Melville, though she didn't know what he did or didn't know about her and Pete, which made her even more anxious.

"Hi," she said, standing right next to Melville.

He shuddered, so engrossed in his notebook that he hadn't noticed her. "Oh, oh hi. Hi Prilly," he stammered, as he closed his notebook and slipped it into an old backpack beside him.

Suddenly with no idea what to say or do Prilly said, "Oh, well I noticed you were here so I just wanted to say hi. I have some work to do, so I'm going to go sit down over there," while pointing to the overcrowded back of the teahouse; there wasn't a free seat in sight. Melville didn't notice her mistake. As she started to turn around he said, "You can sit here if you want."

"Oh, sure, thanks," she said as she pulled out a chair, which made several squeaking noises. She placed her latte on the wobbly table. Nervous to begin with, her slippery hands knocked the mug a bit, and some of her drink spilled on the table.

"Oh, that's ok," Melville said as he placed his napkin over the spill.

"Thanks," she said, sitting down. She stared straight into Melville's eyes, causing him to look down at his hands. "What are you up to?"

"I'm waiting for Pete. Aren't you?" he queried.

Melville didn't know they had broken up. Prilly's heart raced with excitement. She would see Pete; he would walk in at any minute. If Melville hadn't heard about their fight, maybe it wasn't as bad as she thought. Maybe it would be ok. Noticing that the growing silence, she quickly said, "No, no I don't have plans to meet him. I was just in the neighborhood. I'm going to an art show later, so I thought I'd grab a coffee and do a little work while I have time to kill." (She instantly regretted the art show lie as it would be hard to keep up if he pressed for details.)

Before Melville could respond, Prilly heard Pete's unmistakable voice shout, "Hey." As she turned her head, she realized he wasn't alone. Next to him stood a tall woman with long red hair, dressed all in black with a dog collar necklace tightly wrapped around her pale neck. She looked like she was twenty. "Oh, hey you," Pete said, now noticing Prilly.

"Hi," Prilly said, not knowing what to do.

"Hey, I'm glad to see you," he replied. "Melville, Prilly, this is my friend Veronica."

"Hi, nice to meet you," Prilly said as she extended her hand out in horror.

"Hey, yeah, you too," Veronica said, keeping her hands in her pockets. "Pete, I gotta go, I'm gonna be late. I'll call you later," she continued.

"Ok hon," Pete said as he hugged her goodbye. "I'm gonna get an espresso. You two all set?"

Prilly and Melville nodded awkwardly and Pete was off. The next four minutes felt like an eternity as Prilly tried to acclimate herself to what was happening. She had a splitting pain in her stomach and was afraid she would be sick. She imagined herself unable to leave the toilet in the one-person bathroom with mobs of tea drinkers pounding on the door.

When Pete returned, he stood between Prilly and Melville because there weren't any free chairs around. Terrified of what he might say, Prilly blurted out, "I was just stopping in for a coffee on my way to some plans I have and I saw Melville so …"

With his characteristic close-mouthed smile that this time made him look sexier than she had remembered, he said, "Well I'm glad to see you. I've been meaning to call you, but … but you know."

"Yeah, yeah I know. Well I have to go," she said jumping up. "Don't leave. Why don't you join us? We're going to a poetry reading."

"Oh, thanks, but I really can't. I have plans. Some other time," she replied as she frantically tried to grab her bag off the floor without knocking the table and spilling more coffee. "Thanks anyway. Good seeing you. Bye. Bye Melville," she hurriedly stammered as she walked toward the door.

"Prill, you sure?" Pete shouted after her.

"Yeah, yeah, I have plans, sorry. Good to see you."

"Ok, bye," he said, now smiling ear to ear.

Prilly hopped in a cab outside the teahouse and went back to her apartment. She spent the rest of the day thinking about how pathetic she was, how sexy Pete was, whether or not she should have gone with them, and whether or not he was sleeping with Veronica. When all her other thoughts started to quiet down, the last one overtook her. She fell asleep on her couch watching a Hallmark movie about a woman who battled her health insurance company to get an experimental breast cancer treatment. The woman died.

The next morning at seven, she was awoken by her telephone. She stumbled into the kitchen and picked up the receiver.

"Hello?" she answered sleepily.

"Hey you. Did I wake you?" Pete asked.

"Yeah, it's ok though," she whispered. She wondered if he tried to make his voice so impossibly sexy or if it just came naturally. "Sorry. I thought your machine would get it if you were sleeping. I've been up all night. I couldn't stop thinking about you. Come over, ok?"

Prilly stood frozen. Like a child climbing a tree who wanted to go just one branch higher but was too scared to look down, she knew it was dangerous. Still, she kept clinging, afraid to let go. After a moment passed she said, "I have to shower and stuff. I'll come over later."

"Ok. Hurry."

*

Three hours later Prilly arrived at Pete's apartment. He greeted her in his boxer shorts, bathrobe, and signature smile. "Hey. Come on in. I have something for you. I wrote you a short story," he said as she followed him into the bedroom. "It's right there," he said pointing to the bed. "I'll get you some coffee while you read it. I worked on it all week."

Prilly dropped her oversized handbag on the floor (which contained a makeup bag, toothbrush, and change of underwear, just in case) and picked up the papers. There were two single-spaced pages. *All week?* she thought.

By the time Pete came back with a mug of coffee, she had finished reading. It was a beautifully written piece about a man who wandered into a graveyard at night to protect the "sleeping dead." She didn't understand at all how this could be for her. She tried to think of it as a metaphor or allegory, but any connection to her or to them completely eluded her.

"What do you think?" he asked, sitting down on the edge of the bed.

"It's beautiful. Your writing is like a painting. I can see it all so clearly."

He blushed, looking down. "I paint with words."

"Thank you for giving it to me."

Sitting there next to him, she felt just as alive as she had when they first met, but now her head was spinning with questions, fears, and doubt. She still didn't know what had happened, why he hadn't called all week, and who Veronica was.

"I've been really upset since … since what happened last weekend."

"Let's just forget about it. People overreact. I'm sorry I shouted at you. I was hurt. I thought you knew how I felt about you so I felt insulted."

Wishing he would elaborate she said, "I'm sorry if I overreacted too."

He leaned toward her, rubbed the tip of his nose to hers, and then leaned back and smiled. Prilly looked down and asked, "Who was that woman yesterday?" and then looked up, waiting for an answer.

Pete smiled again and said, "Just a friend. She's just a friend."

PART TWO

CHAPTER 6

Kyle Goldwyn was not an average seventeen-year-old. Despite his mother's not-so-secret anxiety that he may be below average in almost every conceivable way, Kyle was, surreptitiously, quite exceptional. He was enormously perceptive. He not only saw things that other people seemed to miss, but he saw them in remarkable ways.

At the age of three, an older and larger boy bullied him at preschool. When Kyle built a block fortress, the other boy came and kicked it down while mocking him. One day the boy pushed Kyle off a swing, causing him to badly scrape his knees. After Janice repeatedly yelled at the director of the preschool, threatening to sue if her son was hurt again (she made such a scene that the woman forever cringed at the sight of her), Janice told Kyle, "Ignore the boy. He's a loser."

Kyle replied, "I think he must be very unhappy."

Janice rolled her eyes and feared that Kyle was a wimp. When he was eight years old, a discussion about Christmas in his third grade class prompted him to ask his mother why Jesus Christ was killed. Only partly hearing the question she answered, "That's what the Bible teaches, that's all. You don't have to agree if you don't."

Kyle responded, "I think Jesus Christ must have been very special. Maybe his ideas were so special that they frightened people." Janice was preoccupied with opening junk mail and just said, "Uh huh."

Kyle ran upstairs to his room, where he spent the rest of the afternoon lying on his bed and wondering what made good people afraid. During the next several years as Janice schlepped him from museum to museum hoping to "make him interesting," Kyle began to see the world through different lenses. When Janice got the free audio headset tour so that Kyle could "properly learn about the great art," he always muted it. He looked at the paintings, sculptures, and photographs and tried to imagine where the artist was from, how they grew up, how they came to see the world, and how much of that vision lay before him, lopped off in a frame. This process made him wonder about different cultures and how they produce different kinds of people. He wondered where innovation came from, why some people's work seemed derivative and others stood on its own, unable to be defined or judged. He came to see beauty in her many guises, which so too made him clearly see her falsehoods.

Kyle was keenly aware of people's emotional centers, as if he could almost feel them immediately. A kind soul, he used this skill only to the advantage of others, never his own. This gift of perception helped him in innumerable ways, not the least of which was related to his mother. Of all the things that Kyle could perceive in his environment, what he saw most clearly was when there was a need for silence. Therefore, Kyle Goldwyn knew that the greatest kindness he could show his mother was not to show her all the things he saw, and so he didn't.

Although quiet and not terribly good looking in the traditional sense, Kyle was not considered unattractive by his peers. Contrary to his parents' assumption, he had dated several girls (including fooling around with a few and sleeping with two). He had many friends at school, and more importantly, had no enemies. Outside of school, he spent most of his time with his best friend, Sam.

Kyle and Sam hung out in Central Park playing cards; they went to music stores and browsed old vinyl; they walked around the Village, talking about the evils of organized religion or politics (they were both fiercely on the left, though unimpressed by most politicians and surprisingly missing the idealism often characterized by leftie youth); they went to parties at friends' houses or met girls at the movies; and most often, they went to Sam's place and watched movies. Kyle frequently crashed on a small futon in Sam's room. Sam lived in a tiny, two-bedroom apartment with his mother, Melanie, a paralegal at a Wall Street law firm. She had long blonde hair, and Kyle thought she was incredibly beautiful and looked far too young to be a mother, though he knew not to mention this to Sam.

Sometimes they stopped by the NYU dorms to see Kyle's cousin, Natashya. Neither Kyle nor Natashya ever told their parents, but they had become close friends during those brutal family vacation weeks. They texted every week (sometimes daily) and hung out at least once a month since Natashya (Tash as Kyle and Kyle alone called her) moved to New York. When one of them had a problem they needed to talk about, they met at their favorite boisterous deli, where they always waited until a booth opened up. They shared a platter of blueberry cheese blintzes and a pot of weak coffee, which they always complained about. Although she looked naïve with a freckled face and preppy clothes that stood out in the artsy punk crowds in her neighborhood, Natashya was a rebel. She used to tell Kyle that she was "sexually free" when he questioned why she always seemed to be "hooking up with some random guy." In response, she teased him that he was just uptight because they were cousins. He thought that she was a little too free. He feared that she didn't know how foolish she could look. Natashya also had a fake ID that she used to buy beer for Kyle and Sam. Kyle and Sam never drank more than one or two cans. From time to time, she also smoked a joint. Sam always took a hit or two but Kyle never did. This wasn't because he was a "straight edge," as Natashya would say while giggling, but rather because he knew that if there were ever an emergency, one of them needed to be sober. He only trusted himself with that responsibility.

Kyle was acutely aware of Tash's propensity to morph free-spiritedness into a lack of consideration for others. He didn't let it bother him until Halloween. Natashya invited Kyle and Sam to a party at an underground club. She insisted that they dress in costume. When they arrived at her dorm, both made up to look like mimes, Kyle immediately noticed that Tash seemed a little out of it. Her eyes didn't focus when she offered them a beer while she finished styling her hair. He figured she had smoked a bit. She was wearing a Playboy bunny costume, complete with a white fluffy tail, white fishnet stockings, and stripper-style white patent leather stilettos. With her innocent face covered in makeup and her very fine light brown hair long and stick straight, Sam thought she looked hot. She had a Lindsay Lohan look. Kyle thought that a long dress revealing one bare shoulder was far sexier than her hookeresque ensemble, but he kept this thought to himself to avoid being teased and called uptight, which he wasn't. Tash was too special to distract the eye in such cliché ways.

"What do you think?" she asked, throwing her arms up in one of her over-the-top model poses.

"You look awesome," Sam said enthusiastically.

"Weeell?" she asked, looking at Kyle.

"I think you're more beautiful than you know," he answered.

She smiled brightly and said, "Let's roll; cabs will be tough tonight."

Three hours later Kyle and Sam were getting bored. The large red club decked out in an excess of black streamers and hanging paper skeletons was massively crowded, and over time, the heavy synthesizer sounds of the techno music grated on their nerves.

"Come on, let's get out of here, man," Sam said.

"Yeah, ok. I have to find Tash to tell her we're going and to make sure she's ok getting a cab on her own."

"I'll wait here."

"Ok," Kyle shouted as he made his way through the crowded dance floor to the last place he had seen her, which was over an hour ago. He wandered around, squinting when the strobe lights flashed in his face. He stood outside of the women's bathroom for fifteen minutes, thinking that if she were in there she'd have to pass him when she left. He sent her three text messages without reply. Tash was nowhere to be found. Eventually, he made his way back to Sam.

"Hey dude, what happened to you? I didn't think you were coming back."

"Can't find Tash. I don't like just leaving her here. She's probably wasted."

"She brought us here man. I'm sure she can handle herself. Let's go to my place. My mom's out with that jackass again. We can do whatever we want."

Kyle scanned the room one more time before acquiescing, "Yeah, ok, let's get out of here."

From the subway, Kyle sent Tash two more text messages. Never drifting off for more than an hour at a time he checked his phone religiously all night in hopes of a reply.

The next day at five in the afternoon, Natashya finally texted:

"HEY. SORRY 2 WORRY. MET A FRIEND. HOPE YOU HAD FUN. HUGS, T."

Kyle wasn't the type to get angry and certainly not one to hold a grudge, but something in him shifted ever so slightly that night. He never mentioned it to her or to anyone.

*

Halloween proved to be a turning point for Pete and Prilly too. They had been inseparable since the day Prilly returned to Pete's apartment. She stayed in his apartment from Friday night until Monday morning every week, as well as most weeknights. They made romantics dinners, read poetry, and went to movies. They listened to music, drank cheap wine, and made love without ever saying the word love. There were only two problems, both of which Pete seemed oblivious to.

First, Prilly's commitment to her work was dwindling because of her preoccupation with Pete (combined with utter exhaustion, also caused by her preoccupation with Pete). She had yet to adjust to her routine of racing to and from Pete's and was often late to work. In an effort to spend as much time with him as possible, she tried to rush out of work at the end of the day, and she no longer checked her email over the weekend. In short, she was working far fewer hours. Tired and distracted, when she was at work she wasn't terribly productive. She knew that she wasn't getting as much done as she used to, but felt it was a small price to pay for finally living a *big life*. At the heart of it, though she would never say it aloud, she feared no one else could make her feel the way Pete did.

Second, she existed on the edge of worry all the time. She didn't trust Pete. She spent many nights lying awake in bed replaying everything he had said (and not said) that particular day. Every comment became suspect. She was consumed by questions like: *What is the message he is sending me? Is our relationship fizzling? Is he happy? Is there someone else?* That last question never quieted down and slipped into her mind at the most inconvenient times, like when she was in meetings with Janice, talking on the phone with her family, or looking in the mirror searching for flaws to cover up. The louder the voice in her head, the more flaws she found. Pete didn't help matters by continuing to flirt with every young, attractive woman he saw, often right in front of Prilly. Nights dancing at clubs that had once felt magical were now a game of "I spy" gone awry. *I spy a slut. I spy Pete looking at the slut. I spy Pete talking to the slut.* All of the spying was exhausting. If trying to be interesting was tiring, trying to be *more* interesting than every other woman he encountered was utterly depleting. Fearing that many of them were prettier than she was, she felt she had no choice. Sometimes she suspected that Pete knew how worried she was; at times, she actually thought he tried to make her jealous. During happy moments, he said things like, "I'm happy with you…well, right now at least," followed by his signature close-mouthed smile and a laugh. He made comments like, "That woman is beautiful, don't you think? Her bone structure is phenomenal," leaving Prilly to stare at him in astonishment, not sure of how to play it. She once asked him if he was trying to make her feel insecure. He laughed at her and said, "Only you can make yourself feel insecure. That's not on me, girl." She didn't bring it up again until Halloween.

Halloween fell on a Friday. Pete wanted to go to a costume party his friend was hosting. When trying to convince Prilly to go with him, Pete said, "My friend Luke is a wonderful cartoonist, very cutting-edge. He does wonderful things with strong female characters that you'd love. He's a bit of an opiate boy, but hey, everyone's got a monkey on their back, right?"

"What? Opiates as in opium? As in heroin? Uh, no," Prilly said, horrified at both the information and the casual way that Pete revealed tidbits like this. "Not everyone has a drug addiction or anything like it. I don't know about going to this guy's place. It doesn't sound good."

Pete rolled his eyes, and in his most annoyed voice said, "He's not an addict; he uses occasionally but he's got it managed. Not everyone who dabbles is an addict. Don't believe everything they tell you on the ten o'clock news. He's an artist and he's very successful. He's fabulous. I shouldn't have mentioned anything, and then you would have gone and had a wonderful time. Step outside the box, girl."

Prilly wondered if she was being provincial. She loved art, and now she had a chance to hang out with a cool artist crowd. Why was she looking for problems? At moments like this, she questioned what Pete saw in her at all. He seemed to think she was limited, and sometimes he actively made her feel that way. She never quite knew if it was she who couldn't get outside of traditional thinking or if in fact he just had a very convenient way of justifying bad behavior, including his own. Every time she started to believe it was him, he said something cutting that hit her insecurity-center, and she refocused on herself. Even though she noticed the pattern, she still didn't know who was to blame. Ultimately, she wanted to believe it was her problem so that she could fix it.

Per Pete's suggestion, they dressed up as Sid and Nancy. This required Pete to simply spike his hair a bit and wear pretty much the same black vinyl pants and white T-shirt he normally wore on weekends, kicked up a notch with an old black leather jacket. Prilly wore a blonde wig that Pete had in one of his drawers. She didn't ask why he had it, afraid to know the answer. She wore tight black jeans, a long-sleeved black shirt, a sequined black leather choker around her neck, and an armful of silver bangles she bought in the children's section of a drugstore. She did her makeup severely with dark black liquid eyeliner and hot pink lipstick.

"Wow girl, you look very punk meets pop art!"

"What does that mean? I don't look stupid, do I?"

"You look terrific."

In the cab on the way to the party, Prilly thought, *Playing dress up is actually fun. I should forget the nonsense about the opiate boy and just have a good time.* She leaned against Pete and held his hand, bumping her head on his chin as they plowed over potholes.

They walked into the party hand-in-hand, which made Prilly feel like the luckiest woman there. The industrial style loft with exposed brick and silver pipes hanging from the ceiling was surprisingly big. *Pete was right – this guy is successful,* Prilly thought. There were large windows, but unfortunately, they overlooked the building next door. Dimmed red light bulbs in lamps around the apartment complemented the seductive background music. As they made their way through the crowd of thirty or forty people, a guy wearing a long-sleeved, electric blue shirt unbuttoned a third of the way down his hairy chest and skintight black jeans grabbed Pete's arm. He shouted, "Hey man, hey! You came! Phenomenal!"

"Hey, Luke. Your new place is wooonderful. Those pieces, are they yours?" Pete asked pointing to the left.

"Yeah, yeah, I did those ages ago. I'm too lazy to frame anything new."

Feeling self-conscious just standing there, Prilly casually rubbed her hand against Pete's arm. "Oh, Luke this is my girlfriend, Prilly."

Prilly smiled and put her hand out, "It's nice to meet you. Your apartment is great."

Luke grabbed Prilly by the shoulders and kissed her on both cheeks. Before Prilly could say anything else, Pete said with a laugh, "So what's your costume, man?"

"Fuck that," Luke replied. "I'm me, man. I'm just me," and he walked off. Prilly watched him grab someone else exuberantly.

"See, he's all right," Pete said.

"Sure. This place is really cool," she said looking around the room.

"Let me find the bar. What'll you have? Some wine?"

"Sure, that'd be great. But I'll come with you," she said, not wanting to be alone in a crowd of strangers.

"Hey, see that spot on the leather couch?" he said pointing to the other end of the room. "Go grab us a seat and I'll be right back."

"Ok," she said as they parted ways.

Twenty minutes later, after two awkward exchanges, one with a guy who wanted to debate whether or not Mighty Mouse was on cocaine and the other with a gay couple who asked her if she could move over (leaving her squished in the corner of the couch), she started to have a mental meltdown wondering where Pete was. Just as she decided to get up to go look for him, she noticed him walking toward her. He was with a beautiful woman dressed in a long, white, flowing, see-through dress with green petals on it (that matched her exquisite eyes), white face makeup, and very long brown hair with side-swept bangs that nearly covered one eye. Pete was smiling and Prilly already knew what he was going to say.

"Prilly, this is my friend, Clyde."

Prilly felt her insides twitching. She was hot and a bit dizzy. Clyde was even more beautiful than she had imagined. *And for Christ's sake she's dressed as Ophelia. Ophelia!* she silently screamed. It couldn't get worse.

"Here," Pete said as he handed Prilly a small plastic cup of red wine, keeping one for himself. As she took the cup she said, "Hi, it's nice to meet you."

"You too," Clyde said in a voice that was every bit as lovely as her face.

"Clyde's dressed up like Ophelia. It's wonderful, don't you think?" Pete asked smiling.

"Yeah, yeah. I thought it was Ophelia. It's great," she stammered, desperate to conceal how rattled she was.

"Clyde's here with a friend. He's in the kitchen trying to make a martini without vermouth," Pete said as he laughed. Clyde looked at him and smiled.

"Wouldn't that just be vodka?" Prilly asked before nervously taking a gulp of her wine.

Pete and Clyde burst into laughter. Prilly didn't know what was so funny but she felt stupid, excluded, and increasingly nauseated.

"Well, it was nice to meet you," Clyde said as her laughter subsided. Then she turned to Pete and said, "I'll talk to you later," before giving him a peck on the cheek.

"Sure," he said.

"Nice meeting you too," Prilly said as Clyde walked away.

"Hey, move over, girl," Pete said, indicating he wanted to sit down.

"There's no room. I tried to save you a seat but it's too crowded. I couldn't hold it."

"No worries," he said as he sat down on the wide arm of the couch just to her left. "Sorry I got held up. I bumped into Clyde in the kitchen when I was getting our drinks. She told me about some wonderful new band she discovered, blah, blah, blah. I didn't want to be rude."

"It's ok," Prilly softly replied.

Pete leaned in, and with his free hand, touched her chin and kissed her.

They stayed at the party for nearly four hours and chatted with Luke, talked to cartoonists and musicians, flipped through photography books, nibbled on hummus, pita chips, and olives, and occasionally held hands. Through all this, although they didn't see her again, Prilly had a singular thought: Clyde.

*

In the cab ride to Pete's, which Prilly thought of as home, she agonized over whether to say something to him. She couldn't get Clyde out of her mind and she was terrified of blurting something out that she wouldn't be able to take back. Biting her tongue, she sat quietly all the way back, holding Pete's hand as he leaned his head on hers.

When they got back to his place, Pete put some soft music on. Smiling, he said, "Come here." She went over to his extended arms. He took her hands in his and started to sway back and forth. She leaned into his chest and they danced.

Overcome by a wave of emotion, "Did you know she'd be there?" quietly slipped out.

"What?" he asked, leaning back, still holding onto her hands.

"Clyde. Did you know she was going to be there? Because if you ..."

He cut her off. "This is what you're thinking about?" he said as he let go of her hands. "This is what you're thinking about while we're having this wonderful night?" he asked in a disgusted tone as he walked into the kitchen.

Mad at herself for ruining the moment and mad at him, she stood there and said in a louder voice, "Well, if you knew she was going to be there, I just think you should have warned me."

"Oh fuck, Prilly," he said as he opened the refrigerator and looked at the nearly empty shelves. "What's the difference? No, I didn't know she was gonna be there. I mean, I guess I knew it was pooossible. She knows Luke, she knows lots of people I know, but she didn't teeell me she was going to be there or anything." He shut the refrigerator door a little too forcefully.

"Well, I just felt caught off guard. I think you should have told me she might be there."

Now filling a glass with tap water he said, "I was there with you. She was there with some guy. What's the difference? I wanted to avoid this. I didn't see any reason to get you all freaked out when, for all I knew, she wouldn't even be there. I know how insecure you are about this," he said in a hostile tone as he shut off the tap and started drinking.

"Fuck you. I would never bring you to a party where my ex might be without warning you. You disappear for ages and then bang, I'm faced with you and your ex."

"Fuck me? Fuck *me*?" he yelled, staring at her through the cutout wall. "Fuck you!"

Prilly frantically grabbed her overnight bag from the floor and stormed into the bathroom where she shoved her makeup and toothbrush into the bag and left the apartment in a frenzy, slamming the door behind her.

*

Prilly was falling over herself as she tried to rush down the stairs and quickly exit Pete's building. Her insides were racing and she felt as if she were on fire. As she flung the building door open and felt a wave of cold air smack her face, she heard, "Wait … Prill, wait."

She turned to see Pete standing there. "Don't go like this. Let's not end things like this."

She stood motionless trying to resist both the urge to tell him to go to hell and the urge to run into his arms. She wanted to leave as a sign of pride, but was afraid that if she did, it might be for good. So she just stood.

"Hey, come on. It's cold out there. Come back inside. I'm sorry I shouted. Come inside."

Prilly stepped back into the building and followed Pete to his apartment. But there was no going back.

CHAPTER 7

Over the next six weeks, Prilly started to unravel. She was consumed by jealous impulses. When Pete was in the shower, she glanced at his Blackberry. When glances didn't suffice, she scrolled through his emails, texts, and phone logs. Sometimes when his apartment phone rang, she answered it. Knowing that would probably bother him, she never mentioned those calls. To compensate for her fears, she tried to spend as much time as possible with Pete. She tried to be interesting, she tried to be sexy, and mostly she just tried to be there. No longer wanting to run home after work to get an overnight bag and freshen up, she brought a makeup case to work and left two drawers full of clothes at Pete's. She rushed out of the office as quickly as possible and raced to meet him. Every time she caught him chatting up another woman, she found a way to punish him without telling him why.

One Friday night when she arrived at the teahouse, he was sitting and reading something he had written to some woman. Prilly went out of her way to be rude to the woman, who took the hint and left abruptly. Pete smirked and said, "Hey girl, she noticed my drawing and asked what it was, so we ended up having a nice little chat and I read her something. That's all."

Prilly responded, "I don't care." She put on a happy face that night and then went out of her way to be disagreeable for the rest of the weekend. She refused to go to a house party he wanted to pop in on, she told him the art at a gallery they went to was ugly after he said he loved it, and she made enough noise in the mornings to disrupt his sleep without appearing like she was trying to wake him. Worse than anything she was doing to Pete was the mental anguish she was putting herself through. Every time the phone in his apartment rang, she imagined it was Clyde, but on this and this alone, she bit her tongue.

Then one Friday afternoon she got a call at work. "Hello?"

"Hey babe."

"Pete?"

"Yeah, of course."

"Oh, it's just that you've never called me at work before. Is everything ok?"

"Yeah, everything is fine. Listen, I need to ask you to spend the night at your place. I have a situation I need to deal with."

"What's wrong?" Prilly asked solemnly.

"Nothing girl, just got to take care of something. Come over tomorrow night and we'll spend the rest of the weekend together, all right?"

"Ok, sure. I hope nothing is wrong. If you need something, call me."

"Thanks. Bye."

"Bye."

Prilly hung up the phone wondering what was going on. She was filled with questions that all asked the same things: *Is this about me? Is this about us?*

That evening, Prilly returned to her apartment for the first night in weeks. The first thing she noticed was a foul stench coming from her kitchen. She hadn't taken the garbage out in week, and something reeked. As she pulled the drawstring bag out of the plastic can, she nearly hurled. She looked at the bottles under her kitchen sink desperate for an odor-eating product of some kind. Absent anything like that, she grabbed a bottle of perfume and sprayed some in each room of her small apartment. It didn't help. She sat on her couch trying to decide whether to order Chinese food, but she was too consumed with thoughts of Pete. *What is going on with him? Why didn't he say why he canceled?* She became increasingly agitated. The putrid smell in her apartment was taunting her. *I shouldn't be here. I should be at Pete's.* She thought about going down to the teahouse in his neighborhood to accidentally run into him, if he was there. Knowing it was too transparent, she decided to order some food and curl up on the couch. An hour later she was eating chicken in a spicy brown sauce with chopsticks, right out of the container, while watching a Lifetime movie about a woman who had an affair with her best friend's husband. She drank half a bottle of red wine and passed out in her work clothes.

The next morning she went through the motions of her former morning routine: French roast coffee and her favorite New York website. She wasn't really looking for something to do; she was just passing time until her plans with Pete, whenever that would be. She wasn't particularly eager to spend time with him but she was desperate to find out how he had spent the evening. After a night of panic, she tried to convince herself that it must be something benign and that she was freaking out for nothing. *If he was spending the night with another woman he would have made up some excuse, but he hadn't. It must be nothing.*

After showering and getting ready, she sat on her couch and tried to figure out what to do. She was having a really good hair day, and her outfit was spot-on. She was wearing a long-sleeved, black, sheath-style dress with black tights and new mauve Mary Jane high heels. *I look good and I don't want to sit at home wasting it. I want Pete to see me before the end of the day when I'll undoubtedly be more haggard looking. I'll throw some work in a bag and go to the teahouse near Pete's. Janice has been on my case to mark up the drafts of the first three memoirs, and with any luck, I'll bump into Pete while I still look good.*

An hour later and a block away from the teahouse, her hands began to tingle. This feeling had become familiar so she knew it would soon pass. As she approached the teahouse, Pete was coming out. Just as her adrenaline was pumping hard with wonder about his reaction to seeing her, Clyde emerged. Tremors coursed through her body as Pete turned and saw her. She wanted to turn around and run away, but concerned with saving face, she kept moving forward.

"Prilly, hey, what are you doing in this neck of the woods? You remember my friend Clyde," he said as he touched Clyde's arm. "I had some work to do and … and there's a problem in my apartment, so … so I just thought I'd come and get some work done. My apartment reeks. It's unbearable and I need to work. I didn't think I'd see you."

"I was just going to walk Clyde to the subway, but if you wait I'll come back after," Pete said as if nothing was wrong.

"Pete was nice enough to help me out with something last night. I thought the least I could do was take him for a coffee," Clyde interjected, gently brushing her long bangs from her eye.

Unable to stop thinking about Clyde's beauty, Prilly's tremors morphed into full-on waves of rage. Clearly sensing she was upset, Pete said, "Yeah, I'll tell you about it in a bit, ok? Wait for me."

Unable to control herself she blurted out, "No, no I don't think so. I'm not going to wait," and she turned around and walked away so quickly that she twice tripped on her own feet.

Pete hollered after her. "Hang on there," but Prilly just threw one of her arms up in disgust and kept walking.

When she got home, she went straight into her bedroom where she lay on the bed, too worked up to fall asleep. A few hours later Pete called. "Hello," he said tersely.

She screamed, "*Fuck you*" at the top of her lungs and hung up. She waited for him to call back but he didn't. Prilly knew it was over.

CHAPTER 8

During the weeks after her father was hospitalized, Janice received regular updates from her sister. Marge also insisted that Janice called their mother every Sunday. The Sunday following Halloween was particularly stressful for Janice. Her father had been released a few days earlier, wheelchair bound and forced to use a catheter, which, like many other things, her mother had been trained to assist with. Again, Marge urged Janice to visit, and again, Janice claimed that she was too swamped at work. She leaned against her kitchen wall and paused before making the dreaded weekly call to her mother. After hearing things like, "Dad's in diapers, Jan. Diapers," from her sister, she knew it would be a brutal call.

"Hello?" Myra answered.

"Hi Mom."

"Oh, hi Jan."

"How's Dad?"

"Oh, not so good."

"Why? What's wrong Ma?"

"It's much harder for him now, being at home. I thought he would be happy to have his foods again and watch his TV. You know he couldn't watch his programs at the hospital. The other man in his room – he didn't have his own room, you know, and we couldn't do anything about it – the other man in his room would sleep all the time and your father couldn't watch his programs. Scott brought him some headset contraption to use to watch his programs, but he wouldn't have any of it. So ..."

"Mom, Mom," Janice interrupted, frustrated that she had to hear yet again that her father was forced to share a room in the hospital, which she was convinced was just a tactic her mother used for pointing out the fact that she hadn't visited. "Mom, you were telling me how Pop is."

"Oh, right. Well, I thought he'd be happy to have his programs and his food. I made him the noodle casserole he likes so much but he hardly ate any of it. He usually takes two or three portions. This time he only had a few bites. I even put those fried onions on top that he likes so much. I made him creamed potatoes, which you know he can't resist, and Jell-O, the red Jell-O, but nothing. Just a few bites. I made him eat some chicken soup that Ellie from next door brought over, but he just sits in his chair in the living room or sleeps."

"Uh huh."

"I don't think he likes me taking care of him, you know. It was easier in the hospital. There's a nurse coming to the house once a day to check on him, but that's only for another week or so. Her name is Betsey. He can't be alone, you know. So I can't leave the house unless Betsey is here, or your sister and Scott. And he's so stubborn, you know your father."

"Do you need money Mom? I might be able to get a little something together to send you. You could hire someone to help you."

"No, no Jan. We're ok. We're just fine."

"You can't do it forever Mom. Not like this. People don't need to live like this nowadays. You can hire help."

"I know, I know. We'll see. We'll see what happens. Each day as it comes, like I always say."

"Uh huh. Right, Mom. It sounds like Pop is just a little depressed. It's a big change. Or maybe he's in pain. Is he in a lot of pain? Does he have the right medication?"

"He doesn't say much, you know. He's on all these pills, and I have to keep track of them. I think he's just tired mostly."

"I'm sure he'll be better soon Ma. I have to go. I have work I have to do, but I'll call you next Sunday. You can call me if you need something."

"You have to work? It's Sunday. You work too hard. You need to take care of yourself Jannie. I worry about you. And …"

Janice cut her off. "I know, I know, Mom. I'm fine, I'm just busy. I really have to go. I'll call you next Sunday. Tell Pop I said hi."

"Ok, bye. I love you."

"Bye."

Janice hung up. She took a deep breath and walked over to a bowl of fruit on her kitchen counter. She shuffled the fruit around, selected an apple, and polished it on her shirt as she walked over to the dining room table. She stared at her computer for a moment and then made a beeline across the hall and into the living room. She manually turned on the television, sat down in the middle of the couch, and watched the last half of a jazz retrospective.

After six weeks, Janice decided this torturous weekly call to her mother was the most unpleasant development in her life in recent memory. She didn't adjust to change well in general, nor did she deal well with family issues. Growing up in a home in which things could quickly shift at any moment, she had learned the value of routine and distance. While it was easy to put geographic space between herself and her family, she became skilled at creating other distances too. Others did not see her discomfort with any disruption to her normal schedule because, true to type, Janice never discussed her problems. However, although they may not know the cause, everyone who encountered Janice could see the manifestations of her angst. Richard sensed he should work even later than usual. He also knew it wasn't the best time to make dinner arrangements with colleagues. He knew this just by observing the energy with which Janice shut kitchen cabinet doors. Unfortunately, unable to see her heart, he couldn't see when it was broken. Kyle knew it was time for invisibility. Only he knew his mother was sad, not angry, even though he didn't know why. So, he spent as much time outside the house as possible, doing his duty of being neither seen nor heard. Her colleagues knew she was "in a way" because she sighed loudly as she walked from her office to the copy machine; she threw the leftover part of her tuna sandwich in the receptionist area garbage without bothering to seal the Ziploc bag, thus stinking up the office; and worst of all, she popped her head into people's offices to say things like, "Watch out, I hear the guys are making cuts, trimming the fat." When it came to these kinds of jabs, Prilly bore the brunt of Janice's wrath.

CHAPTER 9

Kyle hadn't seen Tash since Halloween. They sent each other text messages sporadically. She was busy with finals and didn't have time to hang out, and Kyle was happy to have a break, though he thought of her from time to time and wondered what she was up to. The Saturday before Christmas, Kyle received a text: "HEY STRANGER. GOTTA GO HOME 4 THE BIG XMAS FAM-THING, FREE TOM AM? WANNA MEET @ THE USUAL FOR BLINTZES? MUCH 2 CATCH UP ON."

Kyle responded, "YEAH. C U @ 11."

The next morning on his way to meet Tash, Kyle stopped at the base of the staircase when he heard his mother on the telephone. She sounded strange. He stood quietly and listened to what he gathered was the tail end of a conversation. His mother was speaking in a hushed tone reserved for the most private or troubling exchanges.

"I can't do that. I can't do that Marge. ... I'm sorry. I told you weeks ago that we've been invited to a Christmas dinner with Richard's colleagues. He said we have to go. It's important; it's business. ... Uh, huh. ... I know, I know. I just can't do it. I'll explain to Mom again when I talk to her tomorrow. And I've sent her some money. ... Yeah, ok. Bye."

Janice hung up the phone and stood perfectly still. Kyle waited for the sound of movement, for a sound that indicated she was all right, but he heard nothing. He thought about going to her. His father had told him that his grandfather had been in an accident. Kyle went to his mother that day and said, "I heard about your dad. I'm really sorry."

She said, "Oh, thank you. I'm fine." Nothing more was said about it after that and he didn't ask. His mother was very weird about her family. They never saw his grandparents, although his grandmother faithfully sent him birthday, Christmas, and Easter cards, each containing fifteen dollars. The fifteen dollars, his mother's silence, and quips Marge had made over the years all told him that his grandparents weren't well off. He knew there was more to it but he didn't probe. He liked Marge a lot the few times she visited. She was fun and down-to-earth, and told him funny stories about his mom that he'd never know otherwise. She also swore quite a bit, which he found refreshing. He wished she visited more. He wanted to know his mother's family.

After standing and waiting for a noise to indicate that Janice was ok, he decided to leave. Instead of just taking off as he usually did, he shouted, "Bye Mom, going out with Tash. See you later."

Startled, Janice leapt from the kitchen wall that she was propped against and hollered, "Bye," as he was locking the door. She hadn't caught the name of whom he was going to see.

Twenty minutes later, Kyle walked into the deli and was surprised to see Tash was already sitting in a booth. She smiled and waved as soon as she saw him, reminding him how much fun they had together. As he approached the table, she jumped up and hugged him.

"Dude, it's been so long. Crazy."

"No, no way, don't *dude* me," Kyle said as he gave her a disapproving look followed by a small burst of laughter. "What have you been up to? How'd finals go?"

"My finals were a joke. They were all really easy. I had one twenty-page paper to write, which sucked, but whatever. I think it's all fine," she said, rolling her eyes. "I have sooo much more to tell you."

Before Tash could continue, the waitress came over. "Do you know what you'd like, or do you need another minute?" she asked as she put down a complimentary plate of bagel chips and spread.

Tash glanced at Kyle and asked, "The usual?" He nodded. "We'll have a large order of blueberry cheese blintzes and two coffees. Thanks," Tash said as she handed the large plastic menus back to the waitress.

"What's up? What trouble have you gotten yourself into?" Kyle asked as he dipped a marble rye bagel chip into the cream cheese olive spread.

Tash picked up a bagel chip and broke off a corner, which she promptly threw at Kyle while laughing. "Trouble? *Trouble*? I don't get into trouble. I'm a very good girl. You know that," she said, giggling.

"Yeah, right. So, what trouble have you been up to?" Kyle asked with a laugh.

Tash tossed another piece of a bagel chip at him but it flew past his shoulder. "Aww ... sucker," he said, now hysterical.

The man in the booth behind Kyle turned and looked at Natashya. She mouthed, "I'm sorry," and then Kyle proceeded to make funny faces at her, trying to provoke her to throw another chip. "You're so bad," she said. The waitress returned to drop off two mugs of coffee. "So," Tash said as they poured mini creamers into their mugs, "I met someone really cool. You have to meet him."

"Does he go to NYU?" Kyle asked.

"No, my friend Lyric and I were ..."

Kyle cut her off. "Lyric? Lyric? You actually have a friend named Lyric?"

"Yeah, her name is Lyric," Tash said as she broke off another bagel chip piece and tossed it at him, hitting him right in the face because he was laughing so hard he forgot to move his head. "Anyway, Lyyyyric and I were hanging out in the Village and we stopped in this used music store. She wanted to look into selling a bunch of her old, shitty '90s CDs. She wants to buy this totally overpriced pair of Gucci boots on eBay, so she's trying to sell her old junk. Anyway, she started talking to the guy behind the counter, and the next thing you know, we were all talking. He ended up asking for my email and we hung out, and he's so cute and it's been like three weeks of constant hanging out. He's awesome and you've got to meet him."

The waitress handed them their platter of blintzes with two small plates before Kyle could respond. "You all set here? Anything else I can get you?"

"We're good, thanks," Kyle said.

"These look awesome," Tash said as she smeared a dollop of sour cream onto the tops of the blintzes.

"Yeah, I haven't had these in a while," Kyle said. He cut into a blintz and watched the blueberry cheese mixture ooze out. "Does he go to school? Is he older?"

"He's a musician. He plays the guitar, and he's only like a few years older than me, so it's fine," Tash said, cramming a big forkful of blintz into her mouth.

"Your parents aren't gonna be happy that you're dating some random guy who works at a CD store. Good luck telling them that one," Kyle said with a smirk.

"Oh it's fine. Don't take it so seriously. Besides, why do they need to know, right?" she said with a laugh. "He's having a New Year's Eve party at his place. You should come with me so you can meet him. He lives in Brooklyn."

"I thought you were going home."

"Yeah, I am, but I told my parents that I need to come back at the end of December for a winter session seminar. What do you say? Will you come with me? You can bring Sam if you want."

"Sam is going on a cruise with his mother and her boyfriend."

"Ugh, poor Sam. That sounds heinous," Tash said with a wince. "So, will you come?"

"Yeah, sure, I'll go."

"Thanks, it'll be great. So what's going on with you?" Tash asked. She loaded her fork with another bite of blintz.

"Same old, same old." For the next few minutes, they ate and caught up on the minutia of their lives. Then, seemingly out of the blue and without looking up from his plate, Kyle said, "My grandfather was in an accident. Did you hear?"

"No, I haven't heard anything. Gee, I'm really sorry. Is he ok?"

"I don't really know. My mom doesn't like to talk about it," Kyle said, still looking down.

"You don't really know your grandfather, do you?" Tash asked.

"No. Never met him."

"Crazy."

"Yeah. My mom is pretty upset. I heard her on the phone this morning talking to my aunt. She hasn't gone to visit or anything, though."

"It's probably too depressing for her," Tash said. She balanced her fork on the edge of her plate, looked straight at Kyle who looked up at her, and in a lowered voice said, "Look, a long time ago my parents told me that your mom's family is, like, trailer park or something. I don't know if it's true, but ..."

Trying to spare Tash from coming up with a way to finish the sentence, Kyle interjected. "Yeah, I know. I think she's embarrassed by them or something. Let's talk about something else; I didn't mean to be a total downer." Kyle looked back down at his plate and took a large bite.

"Ok, sure," Tash said, picking up her fork. "I need some more of this shitty coffee. Where's the waitress?"

CHAPTER 10

After spending the rest of the weekend on her couch watching TV, napping, and drinking in her Old Navy pants and a ratty old gray sweatshirt, Prilly pulled herself together to go to work on Monday. She spent the next couple of days focused entirely on work, blocking everything else from her mind by making herself emotionally numb, a skill she learned while being bullied on the playground in third grade. She shut down so she could show up. This also helped in her dealings with Janice, who now appeared downright angry.

She edited the first batch of memoir manuscripts that Janice had been nagging her about. The more work she did, the more Janice seemed to relax. The memoirs came in handy too; she lost herself in the stories of others. One of the books was absolutely riveting. It was about a middle-aged woman, Joyce, who was married with two grown children. She was a university professor who, along with some colleagues, volunteered for a 9/11-related charity. The group was composed of 9/11 widows and other volunteers who worked to help improve the conditions of Afghani women. Joyce ended up going on a trip to Afghanistan where she met a poor man with one leg, with whom she had a three-year, bi-continental affair. She fell madly in love and experienced "the emotional, cultural, and intellectual journey of a lifetime." Her husband never found out. Prilly was captivated.

Prilly's newfound use of work as Prozac was short-lived. She had put in for extended vacation time from Christmas Eve through New Year's Day. The press virtually shut down during that week anyway. She had intended to spend the time with Pete. Much to her parent's disappointment, she had told them she wouldn't make it home for the holidays. After she and Pete broke up, she knew she would be alone; she was resigned to the solitude and never told anyone that she no longer had holiday plans. She considered working to avoid blowing through her vacation days, but when she broached the subject with Stu, he brushed her off and told her to enjoy her vacation. He was concerned about how tired she seemed lately.

Christmas Eve morning, Prilly was in her office organizing some folders to take home with her, just in case she ended up working. Suddenly Janice was standing in her doorway.

"Prilly, do you have a minute?"

"Oh, hi Janice," Prilly said, startled. "Sure, what's up?" Janice walked in and stood behind the chair in front of Prilly's desk. "Do you want to sit down?" Prilly asked.

"Oh, no, I'm fine," Janice responded. Prilly thought Janice seemed odd, even for her.

"I think we should start planning the spring launch," Janice said in a faraway voice. "This launch is important. It will set the tone for the series and I really want to be on top of things."

"Yeah, sure," Prilly said. "What do you want to plan?"

Janice rolled her eyes. "We need to plan the organization of the booth, the signage, author book signings, support staff, everything. We can't just show up with a few books. We need to make a splash."

"Absolutely," Prilly responded. "What if the books don't make it through production by then? What if they're not ready? It's an incredibly tight schedule."

"They'll make it. It'll be close, but a small run of the first batch will be there and we'll have covers and flyers for the second group, so we can promote them even without the books. We need this to go well."

As Janice turned to leave, Prilly realized that other than Stu, they were the only people who had come in to work that day. "What are you doing for Christmas?" Prilly asked. Janice didn't respond, so Prilly added, "I hope you have a good vacation."

Janice softly said, "Thanks," before walking out.

*

An hour later, Janice came home to an empty house. Richard decided to take an impromptu ski trip to their family house in Stowe, Vermont. Janice said she was too busy to go. Richard wasn't surprised since she didn't ski.

Richard and Kyle left early that morning. They would be gone for four days. Janice was used to being alone, but on that day, she felt uncharacteristically lonely. She stopped at a local grocer near her house and picked up some ready-made food from the salad bar and a chilled bottle of white Zinfandel. When she entered her house, she dropped her work bag at the front door and headed to the kitchen to unpack the food. She poured a glass of wine and walked back through the dining room, returning to the front door to retrieve her work bag. She sat down, sipped her wine, and got to work.

The next day, after making a pot of decaf, Janice called her sister's cell phone to wish her a Merry Christmas. Marge was at their mother's house so Janice was forced to speak to her as well. She spent the rest of the day working, exercising on her stationary bike, and watching a Christmas double feature on TV: *Miracle on 34th Street* followed by *It's a Wonderful Life*. During the second movie, Richard and Kyle called to say Merry Christmas. They both asked her to join them the next day, but she said she had too much to do and that they should have fun. She planned to go back to the office the next day and was already feeling resentful of her many colleagues who had taken a proper week of vacation.

*

By Christmas, Prilly had fallen into the depression she knew was coming. She mustered up all of her energy to call her parents. She managed to have a three-minute conversation without falling apart, which she counted as an accomplishment. She spent the next several days lying on her couch, watching women's television, eating takeout, drinking, and fantasizing about Pete. She wondered what he was doing, if he was with someone, and if he was thinking about her. She didn't shower or check her email. She didn't even brush her hair. As the days dragged on, she felt worse and worse. There was living, and then there was living a life worth living. Right now, she was barely living. Over this week, Pete came to represent a life that was worth living, the life she dreamt of possessing. While the tricks of memory are usually played out over time, in this case, it happened more quickly. All she could remember were the wonderful moments of music, dancing, and lovemaking. Nobody like him would ever make her feel that way again. Pete was a big life.

She woke up on the morning of New Year's Eve with a new resolve to reconnect with Pete. She needed to know if it was possible. Her life couldn't be any worse than it already was, she couldn't be any more hopeless, and so she had nothing to lose.

CHAPTER 11

Although it seemed like ages ago, Prilly and Pete spoke about New Year's Eve when they were still together. Prilly made sure to bring it up as a part of her many tests of Pete's long-term commitment. He mentioned a club he liked that hosts a big New Year's Eve bash, and so she reserved tickets online for them, for which he praised her. As far as she was concerned, his affirmation more than paid for the price of admission. In the wake of the breakup she looked into canceling, only to learn that the tickets were non-refundable. Prilly often got stuck on small stuff, almost obsessively. In this instance, while initially irked about losing the money for the New Year's tickets, she soon became enraged over it, with thoughts of those unused tickets cycling through her mind when she couldn't fall asleep at night. But with her new determination to try to reunite with Pete, she suddenly felt the universe had actually thrown her a bone by preventing her from hastily canceling the reservation. It was serendipity.

Prilly transformed from a woman on the verge of total collapse into a laser-sharp vixen with a plan. She planned to get herself looking as good as possible and would go to the club in the hope that Pete would be there.

By the time Prilly left her apartment, she felt invincible wearing a long, full, black skirt with tulle peeking out from underneath, paired with a white, sparkly tank top, black tights, and high-heeled, patent leather boots. Pete had pointed out the skirt in a SoHo store window display. She went back on her own a few days later and charged it even though it was way out of her price range. Her hair was long and sleek and her makeup flawless with dark, smoky eyeliner and pale lilac shimmering lip gloss. On her way to the front door, she gave herself a final once-over in the mirror and thought, *I couldn't look better. Perfect.*

After having a very hard time hailing a cab, Prilly was finally on her way. While sitting in traffic, doubts started to creep in. *What if he isn't there? What if I look stupid?* Worst of all, *What if he's with someone else?* Determined to see her plan through, she pushed these thoughts out of her mind, afraid he would be able to read them on her face.

Upon arrival at the club, Prilly got in the back of a long line of people waiting to show their IDs. It was freezing. She was wearing only a light, black trench coat and black leather gloves. She didn't wear her winter coat, scarf, or hat in case she saw him outside. She didn't want to look frumpy. When it was her turn, the bouncer couldn't find her name on the reservation list. She started to panic, but with a second look, he found her. She was in.

As soon as Prilly walked through the door, she feared she had made a horrible mistake. She had never been to a club, party, or anything like it alone. She didn't know what to do with herself. As she stood for a moment trying to get her bearings, the people behind her started to push past her, making her feel all the more awkward. She glanced upward and saw a blue neon sign that noted the coat-check was down the stairs directly in front of her. She headed straight down, where she then stood in a hallway with gray walls that reminded her of the cheap stucco that lined her elementary school. It was dark with blue lights hanging from the ceiling. She leaned against the right-hand wall, waiting in a long line for the coat-check. Opposite her were women in line for the restroom, which was followed by a men's room, which men entered and exited freely. The hallway was narrow and with people lined up on both sides, she felt claustrophobic. She was getting warm and started to worry that her perfectly done makeup might melt. She felt conspicuous, just as she had as a kid in school.

After finally hanging her coat, she decided to go to the ladies room since it was right there; she wanted to check her face and waste some more time. After standing in line on the left-hand side of the hallway, Prilly entered the overcrowded women's room to discover only two of the three stalls had doors. Naturally, the one that opened up was the one without a door. She squeezed to the side to wait for another one. When she finally got into a stall, the toilet hadn't been flushed in a while and the floor was sticky. It was hard to balance while holding her large skirt up, and she was scared the tulle would drag across the stained floor. By the time she maneuvered her way to one of the two tiny sinks to wash her hands, she glanced in the foggy mirror and assessed that she didn't look as good as she did an hour ago, but she still looked ok. Deflated, she made her way upstairs.

At the top of the stairs, she surveyed the lobby as if for the first time. It was a large, garnet-colored room with black velvet couches and chairs. It seemed to be a mood room of sorts. People were sitting and standing everywhere. To her left was a large room with a dance floor. She peeked inside. It was incredibly loud. Techno music was blaring and the dark room, lit only with strobe lights and blue glow-in-the-dark necklaces around the necks of the club-goers, was absolutely packed with moving bodies. She went back through the mood room to the final room. This large, open space had a slightly less crowded dance floor, with gothic-style music playing. On the left side of the room was a long, crowded bar. Prilly started to make her way over when, through all the other noise, she heard the unmistakable sound of Pete's laughter. When he was really laughing hard, it turned into a cackle that you couldn't miss. Her eyes zoomed to the end of the bar where Pete was sitting on a stool talking to a few people standing around him. Her blood coursed faster and faster. She tried to decide whether she should walk right over to him or if she should head to the middle of the bar, pretending not to see him, and wait until he noticed her. Just as she had chosen the latter plan, Pete spotted her. "Hey girrrl," he shouted loudly. *He looks happy to see me.*

She coyly tilted her head slightly downward and smiled. She hoped he would get up and come to her, but instead he waved her over to him. She felt like she could throw up. As she approached the small group, Pete, sexier than she had remembered, jumped off his stool and hugged her. "You look beautiful," he whispered, his warm breath imprinted on her ear.

As he pulled away he said, "Prilly, this is Jay, Lacey, Kim, and you remember Veronica."

She smiled and nodded. "I was on my way to get a drink," Prilly nervously said.

"Allow me, my dear," he said in his sexiest voice.

She had never met anyone more charming. He turned to the bartender a few feet away and asked for a red wine. A few moments later, he handed Prilly the wine.

107

His friend Jay said, "Pete, we're going to dance; are you coming?"

Prilly held her breath in anticipation.

"No, you go ahead. I'll catch up with you."

As the group walked away, Pete turned to Prilly, leaned in, and said, "It's too loud here. Let's go find a nice spot to sit and talk."

"Ok."

He grabbed his cranberry-colored drink off the bar with one hand and took Prilly's hand with the other. She tried not to spill her wine as they pushed their way through the crowd to the mood room up front. There wasn't anywhere to sit. Just before he was going to say something, he saw a spot open up on a couch in the far corner of the room. "Let's go girl," he said as he hurriedly walked over, still grasping her hand.

They sat down on the small couch and he looked directly in her eyes. "I'm glad you came. I was hoping to see you here. You look wonderful."

Prilly smiled and looked down. "You look great too."

He caressed her cheek and she raised her head. He kissed her softly, and then made a beautiful close-mouthed smile.

"So, how have you been girl?" he asked before taking a swig of his drink.

"Ok. What about you?" she asked, sipping her wine.

"Ah, you know. Chasing the muse." Then he paused, looked down for a moment, and then right back into her eyes. "I've thought about you a lot. I've missed you."

"Me too."

She didn't think she could be any happier. Her fears subsided. She was right to have come, and for once in her life, her courage was being rewarded. Flooded with things she wanted to say but determined to hold onto them tightly, she felt a crack in her armor. Just as she was about to let something slip, she realized they were not alone.

"Oh, hey," Pete said. Veronica, dressed head to toe in black, was standing over them.

"Didn't mean to interrupt. Pete, just wanted to tell you that we're heading into the other room for a bit if you come looking for us."

"Ok, thanks. We have some catching up to do but we'll find you all later."

At first Prilly was thrilled – this time, Pete wanted to be with *her*. But then she saw the look on Veronica's face. Veronica was pissed off.

As Veronica left, Prilly took a big gulp of her wine. Pete gently said, "Put that down." When she did, he took her hands in his and whispered, "Hey you, I really did miss you."

"Me too," she said. "I'm sorry if I've crashed in on your New Year's plans."

He shrugged his shoulders and smiled. "That's ok. I'm glad you're here."

"I hope your friends don't mind," Prilly said quizzically. He shrugged again. "Veronica seemed annoyed."

"No, she's cool." Pete said. "So my girl, what have you been up to?"

They talked about work, music, art, and how much they had thought about each other. Nearly an hour later, their drinks were empty.

"Hey, let's get a refill," Pete said.

"Sure."

They made their way back to the bar in the large gothic room. Pete's friends were hanging out. "Let's join them," he said as he started to head in that direction.

"Ok," she said, feeling exhilarated.

They spent the next twenty minutes drinking and hearing about the group's misadventures on the techno dance floor. Prilly would have been having a great time but she kept sensing bad vibes coming from Veronica. It began to gnaw at her. She did her best to ignore it.

Then Veronica leaned over to Pete and said, "Hey buddy, I need to talk to you," loud enough for Prilly to hear.

"Sure." He turned to Prilly and said, "Don't go anywhere. I'll be back in a jiffy. Go have a dance."

Prilly watched as he and Veronica walked away. Jay asked if she wanted to dance. "No thanks, I'm good," she replied with a smile. Jay and Lacey went to dance and Kim wandered off. Prilly was left standing there, but only for a few minutes. When Pete returned, he was alone.

"Hey girl, sorry about that."

"It's ok. Is everything all right? Where's Veronica?" Prilly asked.

"She needed some air, went for a smoke outside I think. She'll be back," Pete said while looking over at his friends on the dance floor.

"Pete, is there something going on with you two? Are you on a date or something?"

Pete looked at Prilly and smiled. "No, no, it's not a date at all. We all came together as friends."

"Oh, because she seemed kinda upset. She was glaring at me."

"What?" Pete hollered. The music was loud and it was hard to hear.

Prilly leaned in close enough to smell his cologne. "Can we go back into the other room?"

"Sure. Let's go."

They walked back into the front room to discover there weren't any free seats. They leaned against a wall and Pete asked, "What were you saying before? I couldn't hear you."

"I was just saying that Veronica was giving me weird looks, and I was just wondering what was up."

"She's just protective of me, that's all."

Prilly was puzzled. "Protective of you, from me? Why? I don't understand."

"I was kinda messed up when we stopped seeing each other. She doesn't want me to get hurt, that's all."

Prilly was ecstatic to learn that Pete was so seriously impacted by the breakup. It wasn't just her. What she thought they shared was in fact real. Then Pete made a funny face and said, "There may be a bit of jealousy there too."

Suddenly Prilly's runaway happiness hit a wall. "Jealous? Why?" She paused. "Does she have a thing for you?"

"Oh, I don't know," he said in a blasé tone. "We slept together a couple of times, just like a friend thing with no strings, but I think she might want more."

"I thought you were just friends," Prilly quickly said, trying to hide her shock.

"We are. It was just a friends-with-benefits kind of thing. Scratch the itch. You know how it is."

"When? When was it?" Prilly demanded.

"What does it matter?"

"I just want to know."

"A couple of times after we broke up. Didn't mean anything, was just trying to get past you. It was more about missing you than anything else."

Prilly's heart imploded. While she had been devastated, he had been sleeping with someone who looked like a teenager. It was too much to handle.

"I can't believe it. I've made such an awful mistake," she frantically muttered as she started to leave.

Pete grabbed her shoulder. "Not this shit again. I told you it's nothing. It's you I've been thinking about." And then his tone sharpened. "Don't be stupid, girl."

With those cutting words, she turned around and walked straight out of the club. She knew she had left her coat and gloves, but she was too embarrassed to go back for them.

The streets were crowded and she couldn't spot any empty cabs. There were bright lights and she felt turned upside down. The ground was slick. In her hysteria, she stumbled several times and twisted both ankles. Freezing, she noticed a small convenience store and hurried in for warmth. Desperate, she bought a thirty-five dollar, white "I Love NY" sweatshirt, two sizes too big, which she immediately pulled over her head. She headed back outside in search of a taxi. After about ten minutes, she got lucky. She felt like puking and had to open the cab window even though it was freezing. She made it home just before midnight. After cranking up the heat in her apartment in an attempt to thaw out, she took off her boots, tights, and skirt, and got into bed. She tried to cry but couldn't.

Lying in bed, she wished she had never met him. Then she would still be able to hope, still be able to believe that something or someone big was ahead of her, and in the meantime, she wouldn't really know what she was missing. But it was too late.

*

Kyle met up with Tash outside her dorm at eight o'clock on New Year's Eve. To his surprise, she was outside waiting when he arrived. Her parents had given her some money for the holidays. Feeling it burning a hole in her pocket, she decided they would splurge on a taxi to Brooklyn, which she had wisely booked in advance.

Tash was wearing skintight black jeans (so tight that Kyle wondered how she was able to get them on). He thought about making a comment as she got into the cab, pushing him to the other side, but decided against it. He also noticed what looked like four- or five-inch black patent leather high heels. He sarcastically mused to himself how much fun it would be to help her walk later when she would undoubtedly be drunk and stumbling around. Her sweet face was caked with makeup. Her blue eyes were smoky and dark, and her lips glistened hot pink. She was wearing a long, low-cut, sequined, silver top and a black motorcycle jacket that struck him as odd. He had never seen her wear it, or anything like it, before. Right after telling the driver where to go, Tash started fiddling around in her hobo-style silver studded black bag.

"What are you looking for?" Kyle asked.

"Gum, but I have so much crap in here I can't find anything." She giggled and said, "I need one of those lights that you, like, tape into the inside of your bag. Have you ever seen those lights? You know, from the infomercials. They're hysterical." Before Kyle could respond, Tash continued while searching through her bag. "God, I love those infomercials. Don't you love them?" she asked exuberantly. "Sometimes when I can't sleep at night I watch them for hours. The stuff always starts out looking crappy, but by the fourth or fifth testimonial, I'm hooked! I swear! And the acting, that's the best part. It's like watching a soap opera or porn or something. At first it seems totally fake but then somehow it starts to seem believable. Did you ever notice that?"

"Yeah, it's kind of like watching wrestling. Sometimes Sam and I joke about ..."

Before Kyle could finish his thought, Tash cut in. "A ha!" she said as she pulled a jumbo pack of Juicy Fruit out of her bag. "Want a piece?" she asked as she unwrapped two pieces and shoved them in her mouth.

"No thanks," Kyle replied. "Listen, Tash, what's the deal with the party we're going to?"

"What do you mean?" she asked as she zipped her bag. "I told you that the guy I'm seeing is having a party with his roommate. I've met a few of their friends too. They're cool. They're like indie musician types. You'll like them."

"It's a little weird for me going when I don't know any of these guys, and ... and ..." he paused briefly. "I want to hang together," he said, turning his gaze from the cab window to Tash.

As she spit out her huge wad of gum into the wrapper and dropped it on the floor of the cab, she quickly said, "Just don't worry about it. Just be yourself. It'll be fun. It's a small place; you couldn't lose me if you tried. We can totally crash there too if we want to."

Kyle turned away. He leaned his head against the door and stared out the window, hoping that the night wouldn't be too miserable and hoping he wouldn't end up sleeping on some guy's floor listening to him screw his cousin.

Finally, they arrived. Kyle got out of the cab while Tash paid the driver. Standing on the sidewalk, he could hear what sounded like hip-hop music blasting from above. It was freezing and he wished Tash would hurry. When Tash hopped out of the cab, she grabbed Kyle tightly by the hand and said, "Let's go." The front door to the building had been propped open with a few bricks. As they made their way upstairs, Kyle could feel the stairs themselves vibrating from the overly loud music. He wondered if all the other tenants were brain dead or out for New Year's. It seemed like the kind of place where people without New Year's plans would live. The building was musty and foul smelling. Before he knew it, he was being led into an overcrowded, dark apartment that positively reeked of cigarette and pot smoke. The smell permeated the furniture and walls, and he suspected it would linger for years after the party ended. There were bodies everywhere and they all appeared to be in motion. The small apartment itself seemed to be throbbing from the wall-to-wall people and booming music. Tash pulled Kyle through the crowd in the living room. She approached a closed door and flung it open. As the bright lights and smell of pot hit them, Tash dropped Kyle's hand, flung her arms into the air, and announced, "Hey baby. I made it."

There were four or five guys crowded onto a twin bed and a couple of girls sitting on the floor on the far side of the room. One of the guys put his hands out and said, "I was waiting for you, but we had to start the party without you." He got up and crossed the room.

"Hey man, how are you doin?" he asked as he put out his hand.

"Hey," Kyle said quietly.

"This is my cousin, Kyle," Tash interjected.

"Well, I'm Jacob, this is my room," he said as he casually waved one arm around. "These are my friends and that's my stash. Ha. That's funny, dude, I just realized Tash and stash rhyme. So now I got my stash and I got my Tash," he proclaimed as he took Tash's hand and broke out into hysterics. The guys sitting on the bed started laughing too. Turning back to Kyle, Jacob said, "Hey, seriously dude. Welcome to my humble abode. Mi casa es su casa. There's beer and shit in the living room, there's party supplies in here, go crazy."

"Thanks man," Kyle said, struck by how utterly unappealing this guy seemed. He was on the short side and had greasy-looking, straw-colored hair. He was clearly behind on a haircut too. He was wearing light blue jeans and a totally outdated flannel shirt. In the middle of talking to Kyle, he grabbed a plastic cowboy hat that had been perched on the corner of a chair and put it on his head. He tipped his hat to Tash and said, "You look mighty hot, little girl." All in all, Kyle thought he seemed like a loser. He was glad he put the hat on though, if only to reduce the chances of any lice jumping off his head and onto someone else's.

"Let's hang in here for a while," Tash said to Kyle. Kyle nodded as she and Jacob plopped onto the bed. The other people on the bed moved over to make room for them. "Have a seat here, Kyle," Tash said while giving him an encouraging look.

"I'm cool," he said as he grabbed the chair where Jacob's hat had been, turned it around to face the group, and sat down.

"Dude, give Natashya some of that," Jacob said to the guy holding a joint. The guy passed it to Jacob and Natashya put her hand out, but Jacob said "uh uh" with a shake of his head and a smile. He took a big drag, sucking it in deeply, and with his free hand, grabbed the back of Tash's head, pulled her lips to his, and blew the smoke into her mouth. The other guys on the couch exchanged juvenile looks and grins. Tash inhaled deeply, holding the smoke down while offering a closed grin. When she couldn't hold it any longer, the smoke escaped with a giggle. Jacob turned toward Kyle and offered him the joint. "Here you go man."

"No thanks, I'm good," Kyle said.

"Suit yourself, dude," Jacob replied as he passed the joint on to the next guy.

"Kyle's a straight edge," Tash said in between giggles.

"Hey, that's cool. To each his own you know," Jacob said.

Over the next hour or so, they talked a little about music (including how they were all too lazy to go and tell the people in the other room to turn it down), movies (mostly movies aimed at adolescent boys), and even politics (but this conversation was painfully limited). The major attraction of the room was the endless pot supply. After an hour of weed and conversation, Jacob pulled a sandwich-size Ziploc bag out of his front jean pocket. It was filled with little pills. "Come on baby, let's feel good," he said to Tash. He passed the bag around the room and everybody took one, everyone except for Kyle.

Tash leaned in close to Kyle and said, "It's just X, Ky. They make you feel reeeeeally good. It's awesome. You should try one. It's New Year's!"

"Nah, I don't think so. I'm good," Kyle said with one shake of his head.

"Suit yourself," Tash said as Jacob popped one into her open mouth.

"Didn't know you were doin that kind of stuff," Kyle remarked with a serious look.

"Well, I'm a woman of mystery," Tash said seductively before laughing like a child.

The night dragged on for Kyle. He was infinitely bored, and soon, Tash was leaning onto Jacob who was not-so-discreetly rubbing her ass. Between their increasingly vulgar display and the incredible swirl of smoke in the almost entirely unventilated room, Kyle reached his limit. He stood up and said, "I'm gonna grab a drink in the other room, check out the music."

Tash barely noticed him leave, but as he walked out the door, Jacob hollered, "Have fun man, I'll take good care of Natashya."

Kyle left the room mortified for Tash, whom he heard giggling as someone kicked the door shut. Finding himself standing in a dark and overcrowded room full of strangers and blaring music he abhorred, Kyle knew he had made a horrible mistake. He made his way to the disgusting kitchen. It was overloaded with bottles of hard liquor and mostly empty bags of corn chips and Doritos. The kitchen sink was overflowing with beer cans floating in melting ice. There were dirty red plastic cups everywhere. Kyle looked for a clean cup and settled for what looked like the cleanest of the bunch. In search of something non-alcoholic, he opened the refrigerator and instinctively threw his head back in horror at the revolting smell. He quickly grabbed one of several half-empty bottles of Mountain Dew and slammed the refrigerator door shut. The smoke was killing his throat and he needed to drink. He filled his cup, chugged it down, and refilled it once more before returning the bottle to the refrigerator.

He surveyed the room but couldn't see anywhere to sit or anyone worth talking to. Instead, he stood by the kitchen counter and slowly drank his second cup of flat soda. In search of a bathroom, he saw a closed door that he assumed was it. With the music so loud that people on the street could hear it, he didn't see any point knocking so he just twisted the knob and gently opened the door. It was a very small bedroom of sorts with a guy lying on a small couch, wearing large, '80s-style headphones. His eyes were shut. As Kyle went to close the door, the guy looked over at him. "Hey, sorry man, just looking for the bathroom." Kyle stood there for a minute waiting for a response, but was met only with a stare. "Sorry man," Kyle said again as he pulled the door shut.

After using the bathroom, Kyle was able to grab a seat on the couch when somebody got up to go get a beer. He sat there alone for most of the night, occasionally chatting with whoever would sit down next to him. When people started to leave around two, someone mercifully turned off the music. He hoped Tash would emerge from Jacob's room. He hated the thought of having to go get her; he dreaded seeing the pathetic state she was in. Just as he was about to go check on her, Tash stumbled out of the room and made a beeline for the bathroom. Five minutes later, she came out and was heading back toward Jacob's room. Kyle jumped up and intercepted her.

"Hey. What's up? Are you almost ready to go?"

"Oh, Kyle. I'm so glad you're still here. I didn't know if you had left," she said with her eyes swirling. Her eye makeup was smudged and her cheeks were bright red. She hugged him.

"I wouldn't leave you, you know that. You're a mess. Let's get you out of here," Kyle said.

"No, I'm good. I'm reeeally good. I wanna crash here. I told you I wanted to crash here, remember? You can stay too, ok?"

"Come on, I'll take you to my place and you can have the spare room. We can go out for blintzes in the morning," Kyle rebutted.

"Naw, that's ok. I'm gonna crash here, but you can totally go home if you want to. I'm fine."

He knew she had probably stayed there many times before, and that it probably didn't matter whether he was there or not. He detested the thought of spending the night in that rat hole, but there was no way he was leaving her there, not in that condition and with those people.

He sighed and said, "I'll stay too."

"Oh, you're the best," Tash said as she grabbed him for a tighter hug, half-falling onto him. We can still do blintzes in the morning, ok?" she slurred.

"Uh huh," Kyle said with a nod. "Where should I sleep?"

"Stay here, I'll find out."

Tash went back into Jacob's room. Kyle waited for about ten minutes before Jacob came out holding a pillow. "Dude, when everyone gets outta here you can crash on the couch. There's a blanket thingie on the back of the couch you can use. Ok, dude? You all set?"

"Yeah, I'm all set," Kyle said, wondering how wasted Jacob was. He spent the next hour and a half sitting on the couch with a stained pillow on his lap waiting for everyone to leave. Eventually, although there were still a handful of people milling around the apartment, the couch was empty. Exhausted, Kyle took the pillow with cigarette burns in it and lay down. He never saw the "blanket thingie" that Jacob had been talking about, so he took off his coat and draped it over his chest.

*

The next morning, Kyle slowly awoke to the sound of someone stirring nearby. He opened his eyes just a little and was overcome by the sunlight pouring into the room. He closed his eyes and rubbed the crusty sleep out of the corners. When he slowly opened them again, just a crack, he saw a guy standing in the kitchen pouring cereal into a bowl. It was the same guy that had been lying alone in that room the night before. Kyle watched him through barely opened eyes. The guy took a carton of milk out of the refrigerator, sniffed it, and then poured some into his cereal bowl. As he fished around in a drawer, presumably for a spoon, Kyle became distracted by another noise. His half-opened eyes veered to the right where he saw Jacob's bedroom door open and a guy, wearing only boxer shorts, walk out of the room and go into another bedroom, shutting the door behind him. The mysterious cereal man was now on his way back into his room with his breakfast in hand. Kyle lay on the couch, awake but with his eyes shut, for about an hour and a half until Tash emerged from Jacob's bedroom. He pretended to be asleep as she stumbled out of the room wearing an oversized Rolling Stones T-shirt that he assumed was Jacob's. She went straight to the bathroom. Ten minutes later, she was tiptoeing back to Jacob's room when Kyle stretched his arms and made a noise as if he were just waking up.

"Oh, hey. Sorry. Didn't mean to wake you up," Tash said.

"No worries," he moaned. "I'm sure it's time to get up anyway." Kyle sat up and asked, "Where's Jacob?"

"Oh, he's still sleepin'. Knowing him, he could sleep for half the day. He really partied hard last night."

Tash walked over to the couch and sat down next to Kyle. Her shoulders were hunched over as if she were cold. Kyle put his coat on her bare legs. "Thanks," she said. She looked awful. Her thick black eyeliner was smeared all around her eyes, making her look like a raccoon staring at rapidly approaching car headlights.

"You hungry?" Kyle asked.

"Nah, not really. I'm just super tired. I only got up because I was bursting and had to pee. You wanna get out of here?"

"Sure."

"I just have to get dressed. I'll be right back."

Tash got up and went into Jacob's room. Kyle used the bathroom and when he came out, Tash was dressed and waiting, slipping on black sunglasses. Kyle grabbed his coat and they headed outside. Tash leaned against the building smoking cigarettes while Kyle tried to get a cab (which took nearly twenty minutes).

They sat in silence for the first few minutes of the cab ride. Feeling very uncomfortable, Kyle finally said, "Last night I was looking for the bathroom and accidentally walked in on this guy lying alone in a room. I saw him again getting cereal this morning. Do you know who that guy is and why he stayed alone in his room all night?"

"Oh, that's Jacob's loser brother. Melvyn, or Melville, or Mel-something. He's a freak. Jacob just lets him crash there because he'd be, like, homeless otherwise. He's a total dweeb," Tash said. She was leaning against the car door and looking in Kyle's direction, but her dark sunglasses made it difficult to see if her eyes were open. "Oh. I kind of felt badly for him. It was really loud there last night."

119

"Don't feel bad for him. He's a loser. He's lucky to be able to stay there at all," Tash quipped back.

Kyle was quiet for a minute, thinking about what to say next. After a moment passed, he asked, "So who else lives there? How many roommates does Jacob have?"

"You're full of questions today," Tash groaned. "He has one roommate, Jeremy, plus his loser brother who stays there, but he's not really a roommate exactly."

Knowing that Jeremy must have been the guy that came out from Jacob's bedroom nearly naked this morning, Kyle probed, "Oh, did I meet Jeremy last night?"

"Yeah, he was one of the guys in Jacob's room, on the couch. He's kind of a prick." She paused and then said, "I'm super fried. Can we just chill the rest of the way?"

"Yeah, sure," Kyle responded. It seemed like a perfect time to stop talking anyway.

Soon they arrived at Tash's dorm. When they pulled up to the curb, she started going through her bag. She was fumbling around, unable to find her money. She dumped the contents of the bag onto the backseat of the cab. Her money wasn't there. As she scooped everything back into her bag she said, "Hey, Kyle, I …"

He cut her off. "Don't worry, I got it."

"I don't know what happened to my cash. Maybe it fell out of my bag or something. Sorry," she said unconvincingly as she leaned in and gave him a half-hearted hug.

As she stepped out of the cab, Kyle leaned toward her door and said, "Blintzes another time."

"Yeah, sure. See ya."

When the taxi arrived at Kyle's house, he asked the driver to please wait while he ran in to grab some money. He walked into the house, leaving the front door ajar while he hurried to his room for the cash. Janice was sitting at the dining room table wearing a long silk robe and working on her laptop. She hollered, "You left the door open."

Before she could get up to close the door or ask Kyle to do it, he was darting back down the stairs and racing out the door. When he came back into the house, he said, "Hey, Mom. Sorry about that. I didn't have enough money for the cab driver."

"Cabs are a rip-off. That's the great thing about the city: the subway," Janice said quietly, without looking up from her computer. "Yeah, I know," he said as he headed back up to his room. From halfway up the stairs he said, "Hey Mom, Happy New Year."

"You too, honey."

Kyle flung his shoes off, plopped down on his bed and checked his cell phone. There was a text from Sam wishing him a Happy New Year and complaining about his cruise.

Kyle responded: "BACK @ U BRO. THAT'S NOTHIN. I GOT STUCK IN BROOKLYN W T. SHE'S INTO A BAD SCENE. WILL TELL U LATER."

Although he eventually told Sam all about the atrocious party and how Tash was smoking and popping pills, he would never mention the second guy that came out of Jacob's room to anyone.

Lying on his bed, he kept thinking about how Tash seemed to be spiraling downward and about how much it irked him when Jacob called her Tash instead of Natashya. He had never heard anyone else call her that, not even her roommate. He was afraid to even wonder what had happened to her behind closed doors.

CHAPTER 12

Prilly pulled herself out of bed at noon on New Year's Day, sweating in the oversized sweatshirt she bought the night before. She had to pee badly. She thought briefly about just going in the bed, but knew she would regret it almost immediately. While sitting on the toilet, she pulled the sweatshirt over her head, tossed it on the floor, and left the bathroom without washing her hands or flushing the toilet. Shoulders slumped, she shuffled back into her room where she opened her dresser drawer and pulled out an old pair of gray yoga pants and a matching long-sleeved cotton shirt. She changed, got back into bed, and forced herself to go back to sleep.

Two hours later, she woke up with a killer headache. She took four Advil and made a pot of coffee. She stood in the kitchen as the coffee brewed and stared at her answering machine. *No messages.* She took a cup of coffee and a box of crackers into the living room. She sat on her couch, flipping through stations looking for something to watch. Nothing. All of the things that usually comforted her, like movies of the week, seemed to be mocking her. She settled on a channel that showed infomercials all day long. Vacant and numb, she watched for hours, only occasionally getting up to get something to snack on or to use the bathroom. New Year's Day fell on a Thursday, so she had until Monday to pull herself together before leaving her apartment and returning to work. She couldn't imagine ever going anywhere again. She felt dead. She had never felt so empty, so worthless, and so lifeless. She spent the next few days in her apartment watching TV, sleeping, eating frozen dinners, and forcing herself not to call Pete. *I can never call him again* became her mantra.

*

Janice's alarm rang at five in the morning the Monday after New Year's. She sprung from bed and got ready for work, selecting her

123

favorite gray pencil skirt, a white button-down shirt, and a long, black cashmere cardigan. She was in her office before seven.

Prilly arrived at ten after nine. She had psyched herself up the night before, telling herself that things would somehow get better if she could manage to get up in the morning, take a shower, and drag herself to work. She made it her mission to be on time, but a subway delay made her ten minutes late. As she hurried into her office, throwing her work bag on the floor and flopping down in her chair, Janice appeared at her doorway.

"Did you hear?" Janice asked.

"Oh, hi Janice," Prilly nervously said as she pressed the power button on her computer. She was convinced that everyone could suddenly see what a worthless mess she was.

"Did you hear?" Janice repeated, this time agitated.

"Oh, I'm sorry. Uh, did I hear what?" Prilly asked as she typed her password into her email login screen.

"Charles Pruit committed suicide on New Year's Eve," Janice said matter-of-factly.

Prilly froze, looked up from her computer screen, and with trembling fingers softly asked, "What? What did you say?"

"Charles Pruit committed suicide. Jumped out of his apartment window or something on New Year's Eve. Hell Prilly, it's been all over the news and Stuart sent out an email days ago." She snidely finished with, "Where have you been?"

In shock, Prilly couldn't think of anything to say.

"He was one of your authors, right? Didn't you reject his latest book or something?" Janice asked, already knowing the answers to these questions.

"Oh my God. Yeah, yeah, Stuart didn't want to go with it," Prilly muttered, struggling to sound coherent.

"Well, it's not your fault. He must have been a nut," Janice said right before she turned and walked away.

Prilly just sat there. Not a minute later, her computer beeped indicating the delivery of a new email. It was from Janice and read: "Prilly: We need to get moving with our series. I have been working for several days and I have been here since early this morning. You need to pull your weight. I want to see your notes by the end of the day. I will be sending my notes attached to several forthcoming emails. J."

Prilly opened her desk drawer, pulled out her bottle of Advil, and then just sat with it in her hands, unable to muster up the energy to open it. She put her head down on her desk.

A few minutes later, she heard Stuart's voice. "Hey, are you ok there?"

Prilly popped up, "Oh Stuart, I'm sorry, I ..."

"It's all right. I know," he said as he walked into her office, shutting the door behind him and sitting down across from her. "I know how hard this must be for you, but honestly Prilly, the guy must have been pretty messed up. It's got nothing to do with you or with us. He was depressed, chronically depressed. He needed help."

"Yeah. I'm sure you're right," Prilly responded, not knowing what to say but hoping Stuart, though always nice to her, would leave so she could be alone.

They sat for a long moment in uncomfortable silence. Then Stuart said, "Listen, Prilly, I realize this might be tough for you. If you're really troubled by it, you might want to talk to someone. I can get a name for you."

She was startled by his suggestion and wanted to take the spotlight off her emotional state. "I appreciate your concern, thank you. But I'm really fine. I barely knew him," she said in a way that she hoped made her sound together even though she was quite rattled.

With decades on her, Stuart thought of Prilly as a kid in some ways. He also liked her and felt protective of her. "Well you know where to find me if I can be of any help," he said as he stood up and pushed his chair back. When he reached the door he turned back and said, "By the way, Happy New Year. Hope you had a good break. Janice said you two are working on some exciting stuff. Look forward to catching up on it all."

"Thanks Stu. Uh, Happy New Year to you too," Prilly mumbled as he was walking away.

She sat for a moment until she realized that she was still clutching the bottle of Advil. She opened her desk drawer and dropped the bottle, never having opened it. She thought about

Charles. She felt guilty. In her heart of hearts, she knew that the rejection had at least been a part of it. She even understood. Then she started to think about Pete, about the last few days, and about how broken she was. A part of her envied Charles.

Her thoughts were interrupted by another beep from her computer. It was another new email from Janice that read, "P: My notes are attached. More forthcoming. J." Prilly's inbox had seventy-nine new messages, not including those from Janice. She needed to get to work and so she did.

She managed to work all day, catching up on emails and making final editorial notes on the memoir manuscripts. At six fifteen, Janice came to her office and suggested they have a working lunch together the next day to review their progress and to determine what they need to accomplish before Trade Launch. Prilly agreed and Janice told her to make a noon reservation at Nico's, an Italian restaurant two blocks from their office. Janice would meet her there. Prilly didn't have the energy to question how Janice was always able to turn her into a secretary, so she just said, "Sure, no problem."

"I'm glad to see you're still here," Janice remarked before turning her back and saying, "See you tomorrow."

Prilly was about to pack up and leave, but feeling self-conscious she spent another half hour in her office, although she didn't get anything done.

When she got home, she changed into her comfy clothes, made a grilled cheese sandwich, poured a glass of red wine, and headed straight to her computer. She had waited all day to read the news reports about Charles. Worried her Internet usage might be monitored at work, she waited until she was home. While her computer was booting up, she took a few bites of her sandwich and set it aside. As soon as she typed "Charles Pruit" into Google, a slew of newspaper articles and YouTube news clips popped up. She sat reading, watching, and drinking for two hours, watching some clips repeatedly.

She was able to picture what happened that night. He was alone in his tiny studio apartment. There were stacks of books and a desk with a computer on it. He was wearing a white undershirt, pajama pants, and a robe. He was watching the New Year's Eve festivities around the world on his old television perched atop a small plastic TV stand. He was drinking Jack Daniel's. He kept refilling his glass. He had been planning this for a while. Maybe in those final hours he hoped for a miracle, some great change to come and sweep over the defeat. But he was alone. At eleven thirty, he took a final swig from his glass and dropped it on the floor beside his chair. He walked over to the only window in his apartment, opened it, and climbed out onto the fire escape. Without hesitation, he jumped. Prilly wondered if he had intended to wait for midnight but just couldn't make it.

From the various reports, she was able to put together the facts of his life in a way that made perfect sense to her. Charles was forty-eight years old, never married, and didn't have children. From what she could tell, he hadn't had anyone special in his life. He was an only child and was survived by his seventy-four-year-old mother who lived in New Haven, Connecticut. Many of his colleagues and students were interviewed. They all said it was surprising, but that he was a quiet man who kept to himself. Several reporters asked his department chairperson if it was true that he had been denied a promotion recently. The chairperson had no comment. The president of the university made a statement "expressing deep sympathy for his mother" and "confidence that our community will rebound from this terrible tragedy." Prilly thought it was unspeakably sad that a forty-eight-year-old man had only left behind his mother. There may be no one else grieving for him. He was a kindred spirit. She felt increasingly guilty.

She lay in bed for more than an hour that night before falling asleep. At first, she thought about how isolated and disappointed by life Charles must have felt. He couldn't escape the smallness of it all. Then she started believing that's how she would end up. "Hell, that's how I've already ended up," she muttered to herself. She thought about how lonely she had been for so long and how connected she felt with Pete. She couldn't understand how she could love someone so much who cared so little for her. She wondered if maybe he *did* love her and that she had caused all of this. She had shown him that she didn't deserve him. He might not have figured it out until he was so in love that it wouldn't have mattered, but she revealed herself.

127

And now she was utterly alone again, more alone then she could have imagined. If not for her newfound posthumous bond with Charles, she wouldn't have anyone.

*

The next day, Prilly arrived at the restaurant at five minutes to noon. Consumed with thoughts of Pete and Charles, she had barely slept the night before and was frazzled from a long morning spent trying to organize her notes for the memoir series before the dreaded lunch meeting. As she was giving her name to the host, she spotted Janice already waiting at a table across the restaurant. She told the host she was "all set" and started walking toward Janice, who was looking down and writing. Janice looked up and said, "Oh, there you are," as if Prilly was late.

"Oh, I'm sorry if I kept you waiting," Prilly said, wondering if she was somehow late. Janice's first move was always the same, throwing her opponent off balance. Janice was sitting on the booth side of a table for four. She had a yellow legal pad and pen in front of her and a stack of manila folders to her right. Prilly sat in a chair opposite her and placed her work on the chair beside her. There was a long rectangular mirror running the length of the wall behind Janice. Prilly immediately found herself distracted by it, vacillating from looking directly at Janice to looking just beyond her at her own reflection. *I look terrible*, Prilly thought. "So how are you doing?" Prilly asked, as she placed her napkin on her lap.

"Oh you know, busy busy. I'm always madly busy. I always take so much on. I think we should get to work because there's a lot to get through. Do you know what you're having for lunch? When the waiter comes I think we should order right away."

"Oh, um I haven't looked yet. What are you having?" Prilly asked as she opened her menu.

"The ravioli special," Janice said.

"Oh, that sounds good. I'll have that too," Prilly said, closing her menu just as soon as she had opened it. She then pulled a notebook and pen out of her bag as the waiter walked over and asked if they wanted to order a drink. Janice replied, "We're ready to order lunch. I will have a club soda with a piece of lime and the ravioli."

"I'll have the ravioli as well and a Diet Coke please," Prilly said, looking up at the waiter.

"Very good. I'll bring some bread over," he said as he reached to take their menus.

"Well, let's get started," Janice suggested.

They spent the next hour and a half reviewing their notes on the memoirs they had received to date. They talked about final editing, marketing, soliciting endorsements for the books, and many other issues. Janice did most of the talking, and Prilly did most of the note taking, although Prilly felt a strange synergy working with her. They bounced ideas off each other and seemed to have an impressive batch of books lined up along with an innovative marketing strategy. They continued talking through their wonderful meal of spinach and ricotta ravioli in a chunky tomato sauce. Prilly hadn't eaten a decent meal in weeks and realized she was starving for nourishment. It was so good that she used a piece of Italian bread to soak up the remaining sauce in her bowl, but felt awkward when Janice shot her a disapproving look.

As they were wrapping up their work, the waiter came over and asked if he could bring them anything else. Janice ordered a decaf cappuccino.

Prilly said, "That sounds good, I'll have one too. Regular, please."

"So, I think we're in pretty good shape here. We'll just need to hustle and lean on the production team to get these books out," Janice said as she put her manila folders back into her Louis Vuitton briefcase.

"Yeah, I think so too. This is going to be a great line. I will get on that list of reviewers for commentary as soon as we get back to the office," Prilly said as she also put her pad and pen into her bag. The waiter walked over and handed them their cappuccinos accompanied by two pieces of amaretto biscotti. Janice picked up one of the pieces of biscotti and dunked it into her cappuccino. "I hope this is decaf. You never know," she said before breaking out into a high-pitched laugh.

Prilly smiled and feigned a quick laugh, thinking how she would hate to see Janice over-caffeinated. She dropped two lumps of sugar into her cappuccino and gave it a stir.

"So," Janice said, "What's been going on with you?" she asked before taking the last bite of her biscotti.

"Oh, not much. You know, nothing really new," Prilly said while playing with the biscotti. Janice stared at Prilly without expression or waver. Prilly dunked her biscotti into her cappuccino and, looking down at it said, "It's been kind of a tough time. I broke up with someone." She took a bite of the soggy biscotti. It felt surprisingly good to say it aloud. If naming something makes it real, Prilly needed to take something that was the most real thing in her life and make it known in a way she could control. It somehow made her feel less crazy. Although she hadn't had any intention of talking about anything personal with Janice, certainly not about Pete, it felt completely natural coming out of her mouth. "The holidays were kind of tough. You know how New Year's is, and ... and I had thought we would be together."

As she swallowed the mushy cookie, Janice replied. "Oh, I'm sorry to hear that. What happened?"

"Well," she said, pausing to take a sip of her cappuccino, "I don't really know. I think he had commitment issues."

"Oh, I see," Janice said.

"He's very free-spirited. He's an artist. He's amazingly talented. He has that free-spirited artist mentality, you know? I just didn't know if I could handle it." Prilly consciously stopped to sip her drink, wanting to know what Janice would say.

"Those artist types are tough," Janice said with a laugh. Prilly laughed too. Then Janice returned to her stern face, looking right at Prilly. "Was it a serious relationship?" she asked.

"Yes. It was. I thought it was it. I thought he was the one."

Janice offered a sympathetic look and Prilly couldn't believe how easy it was to tell her all of this.

"If they're not ready, they're not ready. If the most they can offer is less than the minimum you're willing to accept, then there's no point. Sometimes it's better to cut your losses and move on. Women who try to change them only end up miserable. They waste a lot of time, and tell me, what do they have to show for it? What?" she repeated, again breaking out into cackling laughter. "Sometimes these things are for the best. You should focus on your career. Then you'll have something to show for yourself," Janice said firmly.

Prilly was a life-long romantic. She believed in soul mates, great loves, and above all, big lives. But she wasn't foolish enough to believe that everyone got to have those things. Being in the middle, her chances were slim. She tried to envision a life worth living without them, without him. She realized that there was no way Janice shared her romantic disposition and couldn't really understand her pain, so Prilly wasn't about to tell her. Still, she wondered if there was something to learn from a woman who had made career her priority but still wasn't alone, still had a family, or so it seemed.

"Thanks. I'm sure you're right. I'm going to try to focus on work and on myself. It's just hard. It's a letdown."

"Sometimes the best thing we can do is to pick ourselves up and keep going. That's what you've got to do. Trust me Prilly, at the end of the day, what do you want to have to show for yourself? This memoir series is a big opportunity for you. You don't want to blow it. You can't afford to be distracted," Janice said sternly. "We both need to do our part."

"Oh, of course," Prilly said, realizing the tenor of the conversation had slipped out from under her. "Absolutely, I won't be distracted. I'm actually very glad to have the work to focus on." Although Prilly was just saying it because she felt she had to, she genuinely felt grateful to have a project that demanded her attention.

"Stuart is expecting a lot from us. I promised him the sun and the moon," Janice said, again starting to laugh. "So now we have to deliver."

"Absolutely. I think we're in really good shape. I feel good about it," Prilly replied with newfound confidence.

"There's a lot of work ahead, but I think we'll get there. We'll pull it off," Janice said with an uncharacteristic smile.

"So what about you? How were your holidays?" Prilly asked.

"Oh well, they were fine. My husband and son are doing really well. We just decided to stay around here this year because my husband and I are both so busy with work. He has a very demanding career too, and it never lets up," Janice said before sipping her cappuccino.

"Sometimes it's nice to stay at home and catch up on things," Prilly replied.

With nothing more to add, Janice said, "Are you ready? I think we need to get back to the office. We have an action plan now."

CHAPTER 13

Over the next five weeks, Prilly followed a strict routine as if her life depended on it. She was at the office every day by eight thirty. Janice usually arrived by eight, if not earlier, and often started Prilly's day by popping unannounced into her office to review her latest ideas. Prilly worked hard, both on her considerable normal responsibilities and, even more so, on the memoir series. She was determined to stay focused while at work. There were long-circulating rumors that the press was in trouble and cuts may be coming, rumors Janice was all too eager to spread. With the economy in the crapper and several years of declining book sales across the country in a world gone digital, Prilly took Janice's warnings more seriously than usual. She had been living off credit cards for years as it was, rotating debt from one low-interest card to another, accruing fees that she chose to "think about later." She was just barely managing to keep all of those balls in the air. She needed her job. Prilly also began to appreciate her newfound working relationship with Janice. Most days they met several times in addition to the countless emails that Janice sent. On several occasions, they returned to Nico's for lunch meetings. Janice always ordered the ravioli, and Prilly usually did too. Other days, they had sandwiches delivered and ate in Prilly's office. Despite the difficulties Prilly still encountered working with Janice (incessant emailing, last-minute changes, and being "assigned" a disproportionate amount of busy work), Prilly also found herself, in spite of herself, enjoying Janice's company. More than that, she enjoyed having a collaborator. It was in stark contrast to the rest of her life.

Weeknights were different – less focused, more numb. When Prilly got home, she ritualistically changed into her at-home clothing, poured a glass of wine, and ordered takeout to be delivered (or warmed up takeout leftovers). She didn't do any real grocery shopping, but she did stop at the corner grocer when she ran out of wine, coffee, or cream. Sometimes she also picked up a salt bagel and cream cheese for the morning, although she inevitably felt guilty about eating it. She spent her nights curled up on her couch eating, drinking, and watching TV. The entertainment tabloid shows and movies of the week that she usually relied on immediately brought Pete to mind, and she knew she wasn't equipped to think about him without tumbling down a dark hole. So instead, she turned to the home shopping networks for comfort. Eventually, she started to feel as if the "home shopping ladies" were all members of a community that she belonged to. She knew the hosts; she knew their styles and senses of humor; she knew when they were exaggerating or even lying (although she didn't care); and she knew that they were always there, smiling and complimenting their viewers. She could count on them. Although routinely tempted, she only bought a couple of items: a new set of sheets for her bed that promised to be as soft as a favorite old T-shirt, and a beige patent leather work bag that gave her a rush in her heart as she opened the box and tore away the bubble wrap. The sheets turned out to be thin and cheap feeling, but she kept them and tried to convince herself that they were better than they were. She loved the bag, which she felt paid for itself when Janice called it "very cool" during one of their lunches at Nico's. Mostly, she just liked watching the programming. It gave her somewhere to go at the end of the day, somewhere she wasn't alone.

The weekends were much harder. She never left her apartment and found it hard to pass the time. She thought about organizing her closet, cleaning her apartment, and even working, but she wasn't able to do any of this. She didn't even bother to shower or dress. All the energy she was able to muster during the week left her completely drained by the weekend. She slept as late as possible, sometimes just lying in bed for hours to pass time. She frequently napped during the day and continued to watch home shopping. The worst part of the weekends was how much time she spent thinking about and missing Pete. He consumed her thoughts. She thought about how much better her weekends were when they were spent with him, back when she felt truly alive.

On the sixth Saturday, Prilly decided to make a change. Unfortunately, it was a change for the worse. Falling back into dangerous territory, she decided to make herself look as fabulous as possible and casually walk by the teahouse. She wasn't going to talk to him, she wasn't even going to go in; she just wanted a glimpse. She knew it was pathetic and a backward step, but once she got the idea, it took over and she couldn't stop herself. Her heart was racing during the entire cab ride, which she interpreted as being *alive* again. Before she knew it, she was pulling up to the teahouse. Her nervous rush of energy immediately transformed into something else. She couldn't believe her eyes. She couldn't believe the timing. Pete was standing outside with Clyde. Just as the cab stopped, Pete, looking hotter than ever, touched Clyde's face and leaned in to kiss her. Prilly was trembling. She heard a buzzing in her ear and she thought she might pass out.

"Drive! Drive!" she yelled at the cab driver.

The driver had already stopped the car, so he turned around and asked, "What? This isn't where you want to go?"

"Please just go. Take me back to my apartment. I'm so sorry but I forgot something. I need to go back," she said in a panic.

"You got it."

As they pulled away, Prilly couldn't help but turn around and look through the rear windshield. Pete and Clyde were just standing there, and she wasn't sure whether they had seen her. They drove over a pothole and she gagged, choking back vomit.

All she could think about on the ride back was what a loser she was. She desperately hoped that he hadn't seen her. Even though she figured he must have known how pathetic she was, she didn't want to publicly confirm it, not again. Not in front of Clyde. After paying the outrageous taxi fare as well as a huge tip because she was too embarrassed to ask for change, she entered her apartment and walked straight to the bathroom. She stared at her reflection in the bathroom mirror. She wanted to remember how ugly this particular shade of desperation was. She wanted to hate herself. She spent the rest of the weekend following her usual routine of watching home shopping and sleeping. She didn't cry. She just tried to completely tune out.

Prilly picked herself up Monday for work. She and Janice were making a lot of progress on the memoir series. That Thursday night as Prilly was sitting on the couch and eating the last egg roll from her takeout, her phone rang. It was startling because her phone never rang. She was on a no-call list so she rarely even received telemarketing calls. She muted the TV and sat, listening. It was Pete. She listened to him leave a message in his sexiest, hushed voice. "Hey there, you … I've been thinking about you. I miss you. Give me a call. Bye."

Although there was an initial jolt of excitement that he called, it immediately morphed into mortification as she assumed he must have seen her that day in the cab. Why else would he be calling now, after all this time? She promised herself that she wouldn't call him, and despite every urge to the contrary, she didn't. It was torture.

As the days and eventually weeks passed, Prilly, still fighting the craving to call him, started to feel like she could expand the bounds of what was possible beyond Chinese takeout and home shopping. She began to incorporate some grocery shopping, cooking, and movie rentals into her routine. One Friday night, standing in her local video store, she found herself perusing the foreign films. She looked at some of the movies Pete had told her she "positively must see" that he couldn't believe she had never seen. She rented a couple of them and bought a tub of butter-flavored microwave popcorn. That night, she made spaghetti with jarred marinara, opened a bottle of Cabernet, and popped one of the movies in. It was a French film about an aspiring novelist and his tempestuous lover. It was beautiful, inspiring, romantic, and utterly devastating. It was just the kind of film she would have watched with Pete. Halfway through both the film and the wine, she thought that the story was reminiscent of the life she had imagined living with him. And then, all of a sudden, the narrator interrupted her thoughts. He was describing how the male lead viewed his lover and he said, among other familiar things, that she possessed a "tinsel heart." In her wine-induced haze, Prilly nearly slid off the couch. She paused the movie and sat upright. She replayed the scene several times. "Tinsel heart. Tinsel heart. Tinsel heart." It suddenly occurred to her that it wasn't just that Clyde was beautiful and had been with Pete that hurt Prilly so deeply, it was the way he spoke of her. He had a knack for making beauty where there was none, just as he made doubt. And he made what was already beautiful sound even more so, like Clyde. She had never been able to escape the "tinsel heart" remark until now.

Until she realized, *It wasn't his original thought. It was a line he lifted from a movie.* Suddenly she couldn't stop wondering which other ideas he had espoused that weren't his own. That weekend, she watched the other films and Googled the many authors, artists, and books he had urgently recommended. Soon she realized that most of his ideas were derivative of someone else's, including his supposed insights about the artists they had seen, like Fairey and Modigliani. There was very little he'd ever said about art or philosophy that developed in his own mind. Even his ideas about love and relationships and being "in the moment" were rip-offs from one of his favorite authors, whom Prilly had never bothered to read before. Sunday night she watched the "tinsel heart" scene one more time and vowed never again. It was freeing. She felt stronger than she ever had before.

*

February was a very snowy month. The city was covered in white, then gray, then white again. The snow made Janice think of her childhood. By the end of February, she sat at her laptop at the end of her dining room table and would sometimes see a childhood memory in between her and the screen. They were usually happy memories at these moments, like sledding with her sister or making a pot of soup with her mother. But the memories always ended with either an awful image of her drunken father quieting their laughter or, more often, the memory of how badly she had always missed him in those happy moments. She wished he would have taken her sledding, even once. She shuddered at those thoughts and tried to avoid the distraction of nostalgia. This year the never-ending snow somehow made it difficult.

One brutally cold, dark night in early March, Kyle was making a cup of hot chocolate in the kitchen. Janice walked in to get some grapes to snack on, and he offered to make her a cup too. Usually, she would say "no thanks," but on that blistery night she paused. "Ok, that'd be nice. Thanks."

She returned to the dining room, and a few minutes later Kyle walked in holding two white mugs filled with piping hot cocoa. "We didn't have any whipped cream or marshmallows or anything," he said as he handed her a mug.

"Oh that's all right, honey. This smells good. I haven't had hot cocoa in as long as I can remember."

As he was walking out of the room, Kyle asked, "Why don't you come into the living room with me and we can watch a movie or something?"

"Oh, well ..." Janice started, but then the smell of hot cocoa wafted into her nostrils. "Well ok. I guess I could wrap up early tonight." They walked into the living room, each holding their mug, and sat on the couch together. Kyle found a showing of the old film noir *Double Indemnity* that had just started a few minutes earlier. They sat silently and watched the movie while sipping their cocoa.

When the movie was over, Janice ordered a large spinach and mushroom pizza with wheat crust. Kyle took a couple of slices up to his room when it arrived. He wanted to try to get in touch with Tash, whom he had not seen since New Year's. They had texted a few times, but he was growing worried. Most of his texts went unanswered, including all of the ones asking her to get together with him. Janice stayed in the living room, watched *The Postman Always Rings Twice*, and ate another slice of pizza. When the movie was over, she went back to her laptop. She saved and closed her work documents, went to Expedia, and booked an open-ended round trip ticket to Detroit.

PART THREE

CHAPTER 14

Kyle was cool and calm in almost any circumstance, but as he sat in the deli waiting for Tash, he felt something unfamiliar: nerves. He'd barely spoken to her in two months, and he practically stalked her via text messaging before pinning her down for brunch. After New Year's he knew she was in bad shape, but he didn't know how bad. He was afraid to find out. He was on his third cup of coffee by the time Tash finally arrived.

"Hey, sorry I'm late. Did you order?" she asked robotically as she slid into the booth opposite him. "There's jelly on this seat, gross," she continued, making a face as she attempted to wipe it off with napkins she quickly pulled from the dirty dispenser on their table.

Kyle scanned her quickly. She was wearing a long, thin, white sweater with black leggings, silver-studded black boots, and a black leather motorcycle jacket. She had several long silver strands around her neck and large silver hoop earrings. Her stick-straight hair looked messier than usual and she was wearing her signature bright pink lipstick. She looked thin, too thin, and when she removed her large black sunglasses, he noticed dark circles under her eyes.

"So ... what's been going on with you?" Kyle asked.

"I need coffee. Where's the waitress?" Tash asked while looking over her shoulder. "I need some fucking coffee, like, pronto."

Kyle put his hand up to signal to their waitress. The white-haired woman turned to them and asked, "What'll ya have?" while looking at her pad, pen in hand, ready to scribble down the order.

"She'll have a coffee, and we'll share a large platter of blueberry cheese blintzes please," Kyle said while handing her both menus. "Thank you," he said as he looked back over to Tash, who was still obsessed with the jelly on her seat.

"So, what's been going on with you?" Kyle asked again. "I guess you've been really busy lately."

"What's that?" Tash asked, finally looking up. "Oh, yeah, I have been really busy. Sorry to be so out of touch lately. I lost my phone for a week, so I was out of touch with like everyone. It eventually turned up at Jacob's behind a couch cushion and with a totally dead battery. I didn't have a charger there either. What's going on with you?"

"Not much, same old same old," Kyle said as the waitress came over with Tash's coffee and a plate of bagel chips and spread. "Thank you," he said looking up.

Tash immediately poured sugar and creamer into her coffee. "It's about time, you old fossil," she muttered as the waitress walked away.

Kyle grabbed a poppy seed bagel chip and dipped it in the cream cheese spread. "I missed these, they're so good," he said as he took a bite. Tash was already halfway done with her coffee and trying to signal the waitress for more. "Hey, have a bagel chip. I see some of those nasty cinnamon raisin ones you like," he said pointing at the plate.

"No, not in the mood," she replied. "I just desperately need some more coffee. It's so freaking cold too."

"Yeah, it's been one big blizzard since we saw each other last," Kyle said. "So, what have you been up to?"

"Oh, you know, same old. School, hanging with Jacob, doin' my thing. Lyric and I have been shopping in the Village a lot lately, you know, the vintage clothes stores. It's super fun. We go on the hunt for, like, a Marilynesque stole or something, and we look around until we can dig one up. I'm going shabby-chic!" she said with laughter. "She's dating Jacob's roommate now, did I tell you that? So we hang out there at the apartment all the time. Jeremy's kind of a jerk but whatever. He hates women. He only likes to do her up the butt! Can you believe that? She puts up with him because he buys her anything she wants and she thinks he's super hot. She's basically like his whore, but whatever. Anyway, what about you? Anything new? How's Sam?"

Kyle could barely put his thoughts together after Tash's barrage. He couldn't understand why Lyric would be into a guy like that, and why Tash would think these guys were cool. He tried not to dwell on the last part of what she said and refocused the conversation.

"Sam is going nuts. Remember that guy I told you his mom is seeing, the cruise guy?" Tash nodded and Kyle continued, "Well he's worried they're gonna get married."

"Does he hate the guy or something? Is he an asshole?" Tash asked before gulping down the last of her coffee.

"No, it's not like that. He's just some nice, nerdy guy. He's been really nice to Sam's mom and he's pretty cool to Sam too. I don't know what Sam's deal is. I think it's more bullshit than anything."

"Uh huh," Tash said, though clearly distracted. She was motioning to her empty coffee cup as the waitress walked by. "Well, it doesn't sound so bad. Maybe he just doesn't want to be crowded, you know? To have another person to deal with," she continued as her eyes widened at the sight of the waitress approaching with a pot of coffee.

"Yeah, maybe," Kyle said. "I'm sure he'll get over it. He's close to his mom; he wants her to be happy." Kyle paused, watching Tash fix her second cup of coffee. "Listen, Tash, I've been kinda worried about you."

Tash didn't look as if she had registered the comment. Kyle took a breath in preparation to continue when the waitress plopped the platter of blintzes and two small plates down in front of them.

"Those smell good," Kyle said, thankful for the respite. He grabbed a plate and spooned three blintzes onto it.

"Yeah, I'm not that hungry," Tash said.

"Oh no. You have to have the blintzes," Kyle replied, holding his fork up as if throwing down a battle call.

Tash giggled. "Well, if you put it that way, I'll nibble a little."

"That's better," Kyle said, smiling. He stabbed a blintz with his fork, put it on Tash's plate, and they both started eating. After a few bites, Kyle tried again. "I've been a little worried about you. You've been impossible to get a hold of and ..."

Tash interrupted him. "Yeah, yeah I know. I've been busy and I told you about my phone."

"Yeah, it's not just that you've been tough to get in touch with. It's more than that. You've seemed different lately. Maybe it's since Jacob, I don't know. I'm just worried about you. Do you really think this guy is good for you? He seems a little sketchy."

Kyle knew if he said too much Tash might completely withdraw. In an effort to keep it light, he kept eating while talking, even putting a second blintz on Tash's plate even though she hadn't finished the first one yet.

"Well, I mean, he's not the forever guy, that's for sure, but he's really into me and I'm just gonna ride the wave. I like having his place to veg in for a few days at a time. It's cool. Don't worry so much. I'm fine."

Knowing that when a woman said she was "fine," the conversation ends or enters dangerous territory, he let it go. "Ok, I don't mean to pester you. Just checking in."

"It's ok," she said, smiling coyly to show she was the same old Tash he always knew. "I'm good, just partying a little, havin a thiiing, you know. It's all good."

Kyle nodded.

"You're so sweet though. Little cousin always looking out for me. I promise I'll try to be better about checking in." She fetched a cinnamon raisin bagel chip and said, "I just can't resist."

Kyle smiled but the smile was a lie. Tash had all but confirmed what he was thinking: she wasn't doing well but she still had enough spunk to pretend that she was.

When Kyle got home, he headed straight upstairs to his room and took his cell phone out of his pocket before throwing his coat on the floor. He was about to sit on his bed when he noticed a folded piece of paper on his pillow. He opened it. Three twenty dollar bills fell out, and there was a note: "Kyle, have to go out of town for a couple days. Order yourself some takeout, Dad will be home late. Fresh fruit in the fridge. Don't let it go bad. I have my cell. Mom."

Kyle put the sixty dollars on his dresser, kicked off his sneakers, and collapsed in bed, leaning his pillows against the wall for support. He sent Sam a text: "YO. WANNA COME OVER

2NIGHT + GET PIZZA, MY TREAT? FOLKS GONE. FINALLY SAW T."

A few seconds later Sam replied: "SURE. C U IN 2 HRS."

CHAPTER 15

Prilly played Pete's message over and over again. She wanted to delete it but couldn't quite bring herself to. She figured as long as no one else knew, there was no harm in deriving the little pleasure she got from playing it, the pleasure she got from allowing herself to wonder, if only the littlest bit, if he really did miss her. She promised herself that, no matter what, she wouldn't humiliate herself by daring to call him back. So now, she had a new routine. She did her best to work efficiently while in the office, trying to keep up with Janice, whom she continued to grow fond of despite the fact that every nicety or bit of normalcy that Janice threw her way was tempered with cutting comments and stacks of busy work. Prilly spent long hours at work. When she got home at night, she changed into her at-home clothes, opened a bottle of wine, ordered takeout, listened to Pete's message, and then made her way into the living room for a night of home shopping.

One particularly *blah* evening as she cut into her steaming egg roll, the telephone rang. The noise was so startling that she flinched, immediately hoping it was him. She wouldn't call him, but if he called her again, she wasn't sure what she would do. She stood over the answering machine as her away message ended and the incoming message began. "Hey you," Pete said in his unmistakable voice before taking a deep, throaty breath. He slowly continued, "Just wanted to see what you were up to, girl. Came across something that made me think of you … I miss you. Well …"

Prilly just couldn't help herself and picked up the phone. "Hey."

"Oh," he said with his characteristic little laugh. "You're there."

"Yeah, I didn't hear the phone but then I heard you talking into the machine," Prilly nervously replied.

"Oh, I see," he said, again with that characteristic chuckle. "Well, I was just thinking about you and so I thought I'd be spontaneous and give you a call. I'm glad you picked up. It's good to hear your voice," he said in his sexiest.

Prilly's heart raced. *What am I doing? Why did I pick up the phone and how will I ever hang up?* "Good to hear yours too," she said sheepishly.

"You want to hop in a cab and come over?" he asked.

"Um, I don't think that's such a good idea."

"But do you want to?" he pressed.

"I want to do what's good for me and ..."

Pete cut her off. "Hey, we *were* good. We were really good, and I think you know it."

"Why are you calling now? So much time has passed, and ... and I never heard from you after New Year's. You must have known how upset I was."

"That's not true, I did call you. I left you a message recently. Didn't you get it?"

"I'm not talking about that. I'm talking about New Year's. You didn't come after me, you didn't call ... nothing. So why now?" Prilly felt stupid letting him know how she had expected him to chase after her, but she couldn't hold it in.

"Well, I miss you I guess. Just thought of you. Do I need a reason?"

"Are you seeing anyone?" Prilly asked with trepidation.

"Oh, not this again. There you go, girl; I call to tell you I miss you, and you ask if I'm seeing anyone else." Prilly didn't say a word, waiting for Pete to fill the void. "Right now, I just want to see you," he finally said.

After a long silence, Prilly said, "I assume you're seeing someone else by now. Are you?"

"Well hell, I'm just trying to follow my heart. I miss you. We had the beginning of something special. Didn't you know that? I know you did. No, I haven't been sitting around all this time waiting for you, but, fuck, so what?"

"Look," Prilly said quietly, before taking a deep breath, "I can't do this again. I know you're seeing Clyde. I saw you with her and ..."

Pete jumped in. "Oh, jeez girl, here we go again. You've got to be kidding. Are you following me or something?"

"No, not at all," Prilly quickly chimed in, mortified and wishing she hadn't answered the phone. "I was just driving by and saw you two a while ago and …"

"Look, sure I've slept with Clyde a few times. She's beautiful, and it is what it is, but I've slept with lots of people. So what? We don't own each other. You're the one I miss. Keep your eyes on the big picture."

"I am, and that's why I can't do this. I just can't. Please don't call me again," Prilly said, trembling as she hung up the phone.

She balanced against the wall for a minute, waiting to see if he would call back. He didn't. She returned to the living room couch and refilled her wine glass. About fifteen minutes later, she ate her lukewarm Chinese food. More than anything, she wished she could have jumped in a cab to be with Pete just for a night, but she couldn't bear the humiliation anymore. It was enough that she was privately humiliated; she couldn't let him or anyone else see it. And she could never look at him without picturing him making love with Clyde and looking into her eyes, beautiful Clyde, not before he knew Prilly, but after. That image was a shameful reminder of everything Prilly feared she never was and would never be, which she felt he had just confirmed. She wanted to keep it secret. Two days later, she deleted the only saved message. She continued with her daily routine of work, takeout, and television.

CHAPTER 16

Janice only had a few minutes at the gate before boarding her flight. While waiting in the pre-boarding line, she called her mother from her cell phone.

"Hello?" Myra answered.

"Hi, Mom, it's me."

"Jannie?" Myra asked quizzically.

"Yes, Mom."

"Oh, hi dear! I'm surprised to hear from you in the middle of the week," Myra said, sounding both happy and genuinely surprised. "Well, I'm actually calling from the airport, Mom. I'm on my way to see you. I wanted to visit Dad."

"The airport? You're at the airport, oh my. Let me call Margie and see if she can pick you up. I know Scott must be working with his big job and all, but maybe Margie can come and get you. Or maybe ..."

As Myra started to trail off, Janice interrupted. "No, Mom. I'm at La Guardia in New York. I have to go in a minute; they just started boarding my flight."

"Oh, well when do you get in? I'm sure I can have Margie or ..."

Janice cut her off, "Mom, Mom, it's ok. I've already reserved a rental car."

"Oh, ok, honey. Well how long are you staying for? Are Richard and Kyle coming with you? I so would love to meet that grandson of mine. The pictures you sent are all on the fridge." Janice tried to interrupt but it was impossible when Myra was all worked up like this. "Shall I set up your room for you? I have some of your father's things stored in there but ..."

"No, no, it's all right, Mom. I've booked a room at the Westin down the road from you. It's only me and I can only stay for a day or two."

"All right. Well come over for dinner tonight after you freshen up at your hotel. I'll make something special. Your dad will be so happy to see you. He's been feeling ..."

"Mom, I have to go. I have to board my flight."

"Ok, honey, have a good trip. I'll call Marge and see if she and the kids can come ..."

Myra was going to continue, but Janice forcefully said, "I have to go Mom. I'll see you in a few hours."

"Bye Jannie."

"Bye Mom."

*

Janice brought her work bag, overflowing with manuscripts, book proposals, and notes about the memoir series launch. She intended to keep as busy as possible. She worked through the entire flight, sipping on a club soda and snacking on whole wheat pretzels. Twenty minutes before landing, a flight attendant announced that tray tables must be placed back in their upright and locked position and personal items must be stored. Janice quickly put her work away and stared out of the window for the remainder of the flight. It was the first time she stopped to think about what she was doing. Suddenly she felt afraid – afraid of the state her father would be in and afraid to face her mother since she hadn't been back to visit in all this time, especially since the accident. She was also afraid to see Marge. Even though they were close, Marge had been stuck with the lion's share of dealing with their parents, and Janice knew it. Since the accident, Marge mentioned this in ways she never had before. Janice thought about all of these things, and she remembered how she had vowed never to go back. Despite these thoughts, as the plane taxied down the runway, she leaned her head against the window, looking out and feeling glad to be there.

After a long wait at the car rental kiosk and a longer drive in rush-hour traffic, she arrived at her hotel. She checked in, unpacked her small suitcase, and transferred her wallet and keys from her work bag into her Prada handbag. Then she washed her hands, brushed her teeth and hair, and put on some fresh deodorant before heading out. Minutes later she was pulling into the driveway of her family home.

When she turned off the ignition, she paused for a moment. She sat quietly inside the warm car and surveyed the tiny yellow house. The paint was badly chipped. The walkway was cracking. Unable to delay any longer, she threw her keys into her bag, walked to the front door, held the screen door open, and pressed the rusty, old doorbell.

The front door swung open. "Oh, Jannie, I'm so happy to see you! Let me look at you. Let me look at you!" her mother exclaimed. Myra was standing in a white housedress with blue polka dots shouting, "Let me look at you" over and over again while grinning ear to ear.

"Hi Mom," Janice said softly, noticing how impossibly old her mother looked.

"Well come in honey, come in."

As Janice stepped into the doorway, she felt as if she were entering a lost world in slow motion. It was as if the house had shrunk; it was a miniature version precisely preserved as if from her memory, a memory she didn't even know she had. As her mother closed the door behind them, she just stood, looking around, and felt as if she had walked into a haunted dollhouse. It was so much smaller than she remembered. She looked to the left into the cramped living room. Nothing had changed – the couch and her father's old recliner looked ancient, the buttercup walls were as dirty as ever, as were the sheer white drapes. The only difference was that their tiny old TV and stand had been replaced with slightly larger versions. In this sad little world, time seemed to have stopped.

"Well, let me look at you," Myra said again, staring at Janice who was staring into the living room.

"Oh, sorry Mom, it's been so long since I've been here, it just ..." and then Janice couldn't find the words.

Myra helped. "It must have taken you back."

"Yes, well, I'm fine," Janice said, trying to regroup.

Myra flung her arms open, "Well, give me a hug, honey."

Janice leaned in and hugged her. As she began to pull away, Myra held on and hugged her tighter. It was a long, strong, complete hug. Janice couldn't remember the last time anyone had hugged her like that, so she gave into it, for a moment.

"Well, give me your coat and then come into the kitchen, honey. Come see your father."

Janice took off her coat and followed Myra into the kitchen. It too was exactly as she remembered, only much smaller. The rectangular Formica table sat in the middle of the light blue kitchen, with a small bouquet of multi-colored flowers in the center. Janice's father sat at the far end of the table. "Hi there Jan," he said, looking up at her.

"Hi Pop," she said, while giving him the once over. "How are you?" She walked over and bent down to hug him, noticing the bodily waste bag connected to him, peeking out from under his dark blue robe. As he started to put his arms around her, she pulled back and instead turned to her mother who was standing over the sink, looking out of the tiny window and drying her hands with a dishrag. "Something smells good; what is that, Mom?" Janice asked.

"Oh, would you look at that Mrs. Jensen? She's so nosey. Any unfamiliar car in the driveway and she finds an excuse to walk out onto her porch and look over. Even when it's freezing!"

"Mom, something smells good," Janice repeated.

"Oh, it's just meatloaf, dear. I wanted to make something more special but with Margie and the kids not coming until tomorrow, I thought …"

Janice interjected. "Marge isn't coming?"

"Oh, she wanted to. She felt awful. It's just that Greg has some band practice he can't get out of. He has a recital coming up, you know. I invited her over tomorrow night. I'm making pot roast, your favorite," she said gleefully.

"Oh, well I'm not sure if I am heading home tomorrow or the next day," Janice said as she noticed all of Kyle's wallet-size school photos on their old olive-green refrigerator, along with some crayon drawings Marge's kids must have made.

"Well I hoped you would stay for at least two nights. We haven't seen you in so long, Jannie. You can stay, can't you?" Myra asked, now turning directly to her.

"Sure," Janice said, taking a seat at the table and hanging her handbag on the corner of her chair as if she were a guest in a stranger's house.

Myra noticed and said, "Let me take that for you and put it in the living room."

"That's all right Mom, I'm fine," Janice replied. Next to the little vase was a large bowl of green grapes, just as there had always been. Janice picked a few, popped one into her mouth, and said, "You know Mom, grapes keep much better if you store them in the fridge."

"I put them in the fridge every night and take them out during the day. If I left them in there, I'm worried we'd forget to eat them," Myra said as she removed a large meatloaf surrounded by roasted carrots from the oven. The room suddenly felt warm and was filled with aromas that Janice hadn't smelled in years. Myra put a slice of meatloaf on each of the three plates stacked beside her, along with one carrot and a scoop of mashed potatoes from the stained pot on the stove. She served Janice first.

"Oh thank you, Mom. This looks delicious."

After serving everyone, Myra retrieved a pitcher of iced tea from the refrigerator and a basket of crescent rolls from the counter and finally sat down opposite her husband.

"Well, we're so glad you're here, Jannie, aren't we?" Myra said, looking over to her husband.

"We sure are," Janice's father said, as he mustered up a half smile.

"It's a blessing, a real blessing. Thank you Lord for this bounty and bringing our Jannie home. Well, let's start eating," Myra said. "Jannie, can I pour you some iced tea?" Myra asked, lifting the pitcher.

"Yes, thank you," Janice said, raising her glass. "This really smells good. I haven't had meatloaf in as long as I can remember," she continued. "You still do the tomato sauce strip on top the same way," she said as she took her first bite.

"Why mess with a classic, I always say," her mother replied.

"It's very good Ma," Janice said with a full mouth.

After a few minutes of eating in silence, Myra said, "So, tell us about the big city. How are Richard and Kyle?"

"They're fine. Kyle is doing very well in school. He is a hard worker and he's very gifted. Richard is doing extremely well at work. He's very busy, we both are. Everything is fine," she said, taking another bite of buttery potatoes.

"Tell us about your work, Jannie. It sounds so exciting, making books," Myra said, smiling at her daughter.

"Well I don't exactly make the books, but ..."

"Oh," Myra said, embarrassed. "I meant ..."

"No, it's ok Ma, I know what you mean. It is exciting. It's very exciting actually. I have been given a lot of new responsibilities. It's very demanding but it's worth it. I'm publishing a new line of memoirs. The press has never done anything like this and the whole project was my idea, my work, everything. It's going to be a very big hit. The series is scheduled to premiere in less than two months, so I've really been under a lot of pressure."

"Oh, well, that sounds very impressive. My, isn't that impressive?" Myra said, beaming and looking from Janice to her husband.

"Yes, it sure is," Janice's father said.

Silence fell over the table again, and the three focused on their dinner. Finally, Myra asked, "So, I was surprised to get your phone call. We were so happy you were coming to visit. What made you decide to come so last minute?"

"Oh, I hope I didn't put you out," Janice began.

"No, no dear, not at all. We are very happy you came, very happy. I was just taken aback."

"Well, I've been working so hard on my memoir series and ... and there is a potential author in Detroit whom I've been having trouble signing, so I thought I would come and meet with him in person."

"Oh, I see," Myra said, a bit deflated.

"So it was a chance to see you and Dad, which I've been meaning to do" Janice regretted the lie that made it sound as if visiting them was just another item on her to-do list, but she couldn't backtrack.

"We're just glad you had time to come and see us. So you'll take care of your business tomorrow and then come over for a big family dinner. We can celebrate all of your wonderful accomplishments," Myra said.

"That sounds great Ma," Janice said, feeling uncomfortable.

When they finished eating, Myra cleared the dishes and put on a pot of decaffeinated coffee. "I made a pound cake."

"Thanks Mom, but I'm stuffed and I'm really tired. I think I should get back to my hotel," Janice said.

"Oh, won't you have just a little slice, honey? I made that lemon icing you like," Myra said, turning to Janice and holding a plate with a small iced loaf on it.

Janice felt terribly bloated already, but said, "Sure, I'll stay for a sliver. It looks great, Mom."

"Some decaf?" Myra asked, holding out the pot.

"Sure. Thank you."

Fifteen minutes later Janice got up and walked over to her father. She leaned in and gave him a little hug. "Night Pop. See you tomorrow."

She grabbed her bag and headed for the door, followed by her mother.

"Are you sure you don't want to bring a snack back to your hotel? I can fix you something real quick," Myra insisted.

"Thanks, but I'm ok Mom. Thank you for dinner. Everything was delicious."

"Oh, we're just so happy to see you, honey. We're so happy you came. Your father has been saying so ever since you called. It's the first time he's eaten at the kitchen table since, since you know. I usually have to bring his meals into the bedroom."

Janice smiled. "I'll see you tomorrow night. Around six, ok?" Janice asked as she leaned in for a hug.

"We'll see you at six. Come earlier if your work is finished. We'll be here, come any time," Myra hollered as Janice walked to her car.

*

After an early morning workout in the hotel gym followed by a day of work in her room, Janice arrived at her parents' house at exactly six o'clock. She rang the doorbell and her sister immediately opened the door. "Hey, Jan! Great to see you! Come on in."

Marge hugged Janice as she entered the house, but before they could say a word, Greg, Marge's ten-year-old ran into the room whizzing a little airplane through the air, quickly followed by his younger brother, Tim, who was chasing him. Distracted, Marge turned and yelled, "I told you two to stop running, this instant."

"Come in, take your coat off," Marge said, returning her attention to Janice, who was still standing in the doorway. "It's so good to see you. I can't believe you're here."

Janice walked in, shut the door, and hung her coat and handbag on the coat rack. "Something smells good," Janice said.

"Mom's going crazy in there – roast beef, gravy, peas, stuffing, and all the fixings. She probably hasn't stopped cooking all day," Marge said as she plopped down onto the couch.

"She didn't have to go to all that trouble," Janice said.

"Don't be silly, you know Mom lives for this sort of thing," Marge replied.

Myra came into the living room carrying two glasses of iced tea. She placed them on the coffee table and gave Janice a big hug. "Hi honey, I'm just finishing up in the kitchen, so why don't you and your sister catch up. I bought that fancy port wine cheddar cheese spread you used to like. It's right there with some Ritz crackers," Myra said, pointing to a small plate on the coffee table.

"Thanks Mom, that looks great," Janice said. "Can I help you with dinner?"

"Oh no dear, just sit and catch up with Marge and dinner will be ready soon," Myra said as she walked back into the kitchen.

Janice sat beside her sister on the small couch. "The kids have grown so much. They look great. You look great," she nervously said, picking up her iced tea.

"You look great too. So skinny. You must be on one of those New York celebrity diets, right? What is it – the zone, the ozone, the …" Marge burst into laughter before she could finish her sentence.

"Well, I just try to eat healthy," Janice said, slightly defensively.

"Relax, I'm jealous," Marge quipped back.

"Where's Scott?"

"He felt terrible but he couldn't make it. He put in a bid for a big job downtown and got the contract. They broke ground a few days ago and he's been working late ever since. Honestly," Marge said, leaning in and lowering her voice, "as much as he wanted to see you, I think he's had enough of Mom and Dad. He's been here a lot helping out over the past few months, and I think he needs a break. This new job was the perfect excuse."

Janice understood.

Marge turned her attention to the cheese plate in front of them. "You know you're the only one that has ever gotten Mom to buy this cheese. And I love this stuff!" she proclaimed as she made a little cheese sandwich in between two crackers.

Janice smiled awkwardly and took a cracker with some cheese spread, which she thought looked vile. "Well it sounds like Scott is doing really well. That's great. I hope he gets paid for working late." Janice bit into her cracker, the taste of neighborhood Christmas parties coming back as the cheese oozed between her teeth.

"So, Jan," Marge said, leaning in and lowering her voice again. "What the hell brings you here?"

"Oh, well ..." but as Janice tried to conjure an answer, Marge's kids barged in, complaining that they were hungry.

"Well take a couple of crackers," Marge said, "but don't get crumbs everywhere. Grandma won't like that." The kids walked into the kitchen with their crackers, so Marge turned intently back to Janice. "Sorry, what were you saying?"

"Oh, well ..."

"Mom said something about an author you had to meet with?" Marge inquired. "She even told me I couldn't call you today and bother you while you were working."

"Yes, that's right. I'm editing a new line of books, a big line actually. I needed to meet with a potential author in Detroit, so I thought I could stop by and see everyone," Janice said. She popped the rest of her cracker into her mouth.

"Jan, come on, it's me," Marge whispered. "Give it up. What's going on? You haven't come in all this time and now ..."

They were again interrupted, this time by Myra who came in and proclaimed, "Dinner is ready. The boys are hungry. I think you two should come in."

Marge shot Janice a look that said, "I'll get you later," as they both stood up and walked into the kitchen with their iced tea glasses. The table was overcrowded with platters of food. It looked like Thanksgiving or Christmas. The boys were already sitting on one side of the table. Myra told Marge to sit across from her boys and that Janice should take the end seat.

But where's Dad going to sit?" Janice asked.

"Oh, honey, your father isn't feeling well. Today's a bad day. He just can't make it to the table so I fixed him a tray. He feels terrible with you being here and all, but you can go and say hi after dinner," Myra explained as she sat down, setting adding a bowl of peas to complete the feast.

"Well, everyone – let's eat!"

*

After dinner, Myra cleared the dishes. The boys asked if they could go and play, to which Marge said, "Just be good; don't make a mess." She then asked, "Mom, can I help you with the dishes?"

Janice chimed in. "Oh, can I help you Mom?"

"No, no, girls. I'm just going to get a pot of coffee going over here. You girls can bring dessert to your father. I know he really wanted to visit with you, Jannie."

"Oh, you don't need to go to the trouble, Mom. I'm stuffed," Janice said.

"It's no trouble. I made one of your favorites, apple cobbler. I would have made peach but you know they aren't in season yet. You can just have a little, dear. Besides, I know your father really wants to see you. He can't resist my cobbler, even at his crankiest." Myra removed the Saran wrap from the big casserole dish on the counter.

As she peeled away the plastic, swirls of cinnamon filled the room. Janice suddenly remembered long days spent playing outside with Marge in their secret fortress. They returned to the house, dripping with dirt, to the smell of freshly baked cobbler just out of the oven. Before she knew it, Myra was handing Janice a dessert bowl with cobbler and a scoop of vanilla ice cream melting on top. "That's for your father. You and Margie can bring it to him and have a little visit. When you're done, the decaf will be ready and you can come in for dessert. I made gingersnap cookies for the boys, and I thought you might want to bring a few home for Kyle, Jannie. Oh Margie, there's plenty for Scott too. I'll make him a care package so he can have a nice hot dinner when he gets home."

"Thanks Mom," Marge said.

Janice didn't move from her seat at the table, holding her father's dessert. "Here you go, dear," Myra said, handing her a napkin and spoon. "Everything will be ready in about ten minutes."

Janice and Marge walked to their parents' bedroom. Marge knocked on the door. They heard grumbling on the other side that sounded like "come in." As Janice followed Marge into the small room that had seemed so much bigger as a child, she stared at the old, embattled man lying in his bed who also seemed so much bigger when she was a child. Two small, dim lamps on each nightstand provided the only light in the bleak room. Their father was sitting up in bed, propped against several pillows. Marge took the only chair in the room, in a corner near a small window. Janice handed her father his dessert, looked over at Marge, and then sat on the edge of the bed.

"Thank you, but I'm not hungry," he mumbled.

Janice reached out to the take bowl back, but Marge chimed in. "Just eat the cobbler, Dad. Mom made it special. Just try it."

He nodded.

"So Dad, how are you feeling?" Marge asked, sounding annoyed. Janice thought about how Marge always sounded annoyed on the phone when talking about her father, and apparently, even when talking to him. Things hadn't improved between them despite his ailments. She couldn't hide her resentment over the fact that he was still taking up space in her life.

"I'm ok," he said, fidgeting and trying to get comfortable enough to eat. "How are the boys? How is Scott's new job going?" he asked before taking a bite of his cobbler.

"Everyone's fine, Dad," Marge replied. "So, what about Janice? She came all this way." Marge's tone seemed to offer a suggestion to her father.

"Yes. I'm just so glad you came Jan," he said, looking at Janice and trying to smile.

"I'm sorry you aren't feeling well Pop," Janice said.

He took another bite of the cobbler and said, "This is really good. Aren't you two having any?"

"We'll join Mom in a bit. We wanted to see you first," Janice replied. "It smells good. I haven't had cobbler since I lived here," she said, smiling at her father.

"Yeah, well I can see why you wouldn't want the tastes of home," Marge said sarcastically.

"I remember how much you and I liked Mom's peach cobbler in the summer; do you remember that, Dad?" Janice asked, trying to focus only on her father.

"He doesn't remember anything," Marge said.

Janice's father smiled half-heartedly at Janice and looked over at Marge, as if to plead for sympathy.

"You know what I remember?" he said.

"What, Pop? What do you remember?" Janice asked softly.

"That summer we went to the big fair in Ann Arbor. Do you remember that? This cobbler smells a lot like something they had there. Do you remember?"

"I think it was those apple donuts," Janice said. "Do you remember those donuts, Marge?" she asked. "We bought a bag and ate them the whole drive home."

Marge shook her head.

"Yes, that's what it was, the donuts," their father said with another small smile.

"That was such a fun day, one of the best I remember," Janice said with a sigh.

"You must not remember it then. Don't you remember all the beer Dad drank and him fighting with Mom about driving home? On the walk to the car, he jumped and slammed his hand into that big sign, that big, green, metal freeway sign. Don't you remember? There was blood everywhere, and he was screaming," Marge said angrily.

Silence hung like a shroud. After a couple of moments passed, Janice said, "I remember having fun that day. It was the prettiest place I had ever seen. We had all of those tickets, those tickets for the rides, and there was that rollercoaster. I had never been on anything like that before. And I remember you got us lots of treats that day," Janice said.

"Yes, that's right. I think you had cotton candy, and Marge, Marge you had an ice cream cone, right?" their father asked.

"I had a waffle ice cream sandwich," Marge said.

"That's right. Chocolate," he said.

"No Dad, it was strawberry," Marge said. She stormed out of the room, forcefully shutting the door behind her.

Janice looked lovingly at her father. "Your cotton candy, it was pink right, bright pink?" he asked.

"Yes, Pop."

"Jannie, I don't blame you for not visiting. I know that ..."

Janice spared him from finishing his sentence. "I've been so busy, really, you can't imagine what it's like in New York. I just couldn't get away ..."

"Jannie, it's ok. I understand."

"Pop, when you had your accident I wanted to ..."

This time, he took her hand and looked her squarely in the eye. "Jannie, it wasn't an accident. It wasn't an accident."

Janice sat perfectly still, her hand resting limply in his. "What do you mean, Pop? Were you ..." but she couldn't find the words.

"No. I wasn't drinking, Jannie. I know you have no reason to believe this but I've been sober for a few years now. Your mother finally threatened to leave me, and she meant it. She packed a bag and went to stay with one of those ladies from the church. And, well, I couldn't do it without her. It was a battle but I've been sober." He paused again. "I wasn't drinking that day."

He looked down and Janice moved her hand to really embrace his. "What do you mean Pop, that it wasn't an accident?"

"It's been real hard Jannie, real hard. I don't remember much, but I know what I am and I know what I've done to all of you. Your mother's been telling me for years how awful I was. When I think about ..." He shuddered and seemed to be trying to gather his strength. "She was a young, beautiful woman when I met her, and now she's almost done, she's almost done, and she's been stuck with me and my problem."

Janice could hardly believe what she was hearing. "What do you mean it wasn't an accident, Pop?" she asked again.

"I know what I am, and I couldn't take it no more. I thought I would release your mother, release all of you. That maybe you'd visit her, and your sister wouldn't be so angry anymore. Wastin' her life with that damn anger, like a cancer. I just didn't see what was left at this end. That's why, Jannie. That's why I did it. That's why I walked across that way like that. That's why. And now look at me. Look at your mother. I couldn't even do this right." He paused. "I never told your mother. She never asked."

Janice sat still and quiet with tears streaming down her face. They didn't say anything else. A few minutes later, she gave him a long hug and left him alone. She solemnly joined Marge and her mother in the kitchen. She sat in silence eating cobbler and drinking decaf while they spoke about some shopping trip they were planning for the weekend.

When Janice left the house, she hugged her mother as completely as her mother had hugged her. Although she didn't say a word, Myra felt grateful.

When Janice arrived home the next afternoon, Kyle was sitting in the living room watching TV. She pulled a Ziploc bag of gingersnap cookies from her bag and handed them to him. "I'm tired. I'm going to shower and maybe take a rest," she said.

"Ok, Mom. Thanks for the cookies," Kyle said, confused. He was preoccupied. He had a terrible feeling that something bad was going to happen, and he wished that Tash would respond to his many text messages.

CHAPTER 17

Jeremy Bransfield spent most days sleeping late, playing video games, smoking pot with his roommate, Jacob, and sleeping with his girlfriend, Lyric (or whatever girl he could get up to his apartment). Although ragged and unkempt, he was naturally good looking and tall, with great bone structure and intense, dark eyes. He looked even better when compared to his roommate. Women perceived Jacob as the grimy little pot guy and Jeremy as his hot roommate. But for all his foolishness, Jacob was, at his core, a decent person who meant no harm. Jeremy, on the other hand, was smart, slick, and far more dangerous than Jacob was capable of realizing.

Jacob met Jeremy when he came into the used record store looking for an obscure reggae artist. It wasn't long before Jeremy offered Jacob a "business opportunity" to deal dope out of the backroom of the store. With declining sales, Jacob had been worried about losing his job. He also liked the idea of access to free pot, so he quickly agreed. A bumpkin in many ways, Jacob didn't realize that the deal was Jeremy's true motive for coming into that store that day. Jacob later gave Jeremy a reggae CD as a gift. Thinking he was quite clever, Jacob eventually started putting some of his cut of the drug profits into the cash register at the store, to prevent the store from going under. Despite his profits from the illicit sales, he wanted to keep his job. It made him feel like a good guy, a clever guy. Jeremy just wanted to keep the location available for his shady dealings. The two became fast friends. Soon, the small pot business transformed into a full-fledged pharmacy of pills and powders that Jacob chose not to think too much about. It didn't take long for the two to become roommates. Jeremy thought this would make Jacob easier to monitor. Every Tuesday morning, Jeremy's alarm clock rang at seven. He showered and was out of the apartment by eight, listening to headphones and carrying an old, gray backpack. He spent the day traveling by trains and buses. First, he stopped and picked up bialys and cream cheese from a local bakery that boasted the best bialys in Brooklyn. Then he visited his grandmother in a nursing home in

Queens. When he arrived, she was always sitting in her room at the doily-covered table by the window. She wore a dress every Tuesday and was always waiting for his arrival. She asked a staff member to bring them some tea, and Jeremy fixed a bialy and cream cheese for each of them. They usually played cards or checkers. He stayed for exactly one hour, an hour that his grandmother looked forward to all week. He was her only visitor.

Three times a month, this visit was followed by a series of errands or other meaningless activities. But on the fourth Tuesday, he made his way to a tenement in the South Bronx. There, he emptied his backpack filled with money and refilled it with pills and powders. It was a long trip for a fast exchange. On his way back to the subway, he stopped at a small Puerto Rican takeout restaurant. He bought a large garlic chicken plate, a large order of rice and beans, and a large container of coconut drink. With his backpack on his shoulders and bag of food in his hand, he made the long trip back to Brooklyn to chow down with Jacob. Melville always smelled the garlic from his room. The next morning, Jacob took the backpack to the store, unpacked, and opened for business. This routine went off without a hitch until one cold Wednesday morning in March.

Tash had spent the night at Jacob's apartment. Although it seemed like she lived there, she normally went back to her dorm on Mondays and didn't return until Thursday night so she could attend her Tuesday and Thursday classes. This week, however, was Spring Break, and Tash wanted to spend it stoned at Jacob's. She wanted Lyric to stay too, but Lyric was growing tired of the endless cycle of getting high and coming down. She began to feel that the apartment was like a vortex that slowly sucked time before anyone could notice. Lyric was almost done with "up-the-ass Jeremy," as she had come to think of him, and used the school break as excuse to get out of town with some of her friends. She was ready to sport a string bikini, guzzle margaritas, and go down on a random jock like the good old days. She wanted Tash to join her but Tash was living in another world.

Tash was usually able to pull it together enough to go through the motions of attending class, but she had become more of a squatter than a college student. And so, this was the first Wednesday morning that Tash found herself in Jacob's apartment. Jacob got up and ready for work as usual, trying not to wake her. As he was zipping up Jeremy's backpack, Tash rolled over and sleepily said, "Hey. What's going on?"

"I gotta go to work, you know that, babe. Go back to sleep. You can just crash here today, and we'll hang when I get back."

Tash was groggy but she rubbed her eyes and tried to focus on what was happening. It occurred to her that with Jacob at work, she would be stuck in the apartment all day with Jeremy.

"Wait! Wait for me. I'll come with you," she said, sitting up and stretching her arms toward the ceiling.

"Babe, that's sweet but I gotta go and you'll take forever. Besides, you'll be bored out of your mind," Jacob retorted while putting his jacket on.

Tash leapt from the bed, revealing a hot pink tank top and white cotton underwear. "I'll be ready super fast. I can hang with you in the store, and if it gets boring, I can bum around the Village. Besides, I need to stop by my dorm at some point to pick up a few things. Just hold up for a couple minutes."

Jacob didn't think Jeremy would be happy if Tash tagged along that day. He had been pissed when he had to share the takeout with her the night before, but looking at her and how sexy she was, he found it hard to say no and figured it wasn't a big deal. "You gotta hurry, I can't be late."

"No problem. Give me five minutes," she said as pulled her jeans on.

Thirty minutes later, they were on the train with two coffees purchased from a street vendor. Despite rush hour, they managed to snag two seats when some yuppies got off. Tash leaned on Jacob's shoulder the whole ride. Sometimes she started to drift off, but a bump or announcement from the conductor always jarred her awake. Just before they arrived at their stop, Tash nodded off again, lost her grip on her coffee cup, and spilled it in Jacob's lap. He jumped up, screaming, "Oh shit!" Tash hopped up and tried to help. She found an old tissue in her pocket and manically wiped his pants, bumping into the other passengers as the train screeched into the station. She grabbed Jacob's coffee cup as they hurriedly tried to make their way off the bustling train. In all the commotion, Jacob left the backpack on his seat. He realized what he had done as soon as he was standing on the platform, watching the train go by. It happened so quickly. He could only stand there, with his heart racing.

"Holy shit, holy shit," he screamed. He threw his arms up in the air and then rested his hands on his head in disbelief.

Totally unaware, Tash asked, "What's wrong? Why are you freaking out?"

"The bag, the bag," he said, breathing heavily.

"You left your bag on the train?" Tash asked, rolling her eyes as if this was somehow an inconvenience for her. "Well, let's go find someone who works here and ask what you can do. They can probably call the driver or something, or maybe there's a lost and found or something."

Jacob just stood, staring down the dark tunnel that unfurled before him. It was crowded and loud, but he felt utterly alone. Everything was happening in slow motion. He could barely make out the words Tash was saying.

"Jacob, don't worry about it. I'm sure we'll get the bag back," Tash said, tapping his back. "Chill out."

"I'm dead. I'm so dead," he muttered.

"Come on, let's get out of here," Tash said.

"I gotta get to the store and call Jeremy."

"Why? Don't you think you should talk to someone here?" she asked. "Maybe they can get your bag."

"Come on, I gotta go and call Jeremy."

"Well, you can use my cell," she said, as she dug through her pocketbook.

"No, I'll call from the store. Let's get out of here. I'll explain it on the way."

*

Jacob sat solemnly in the backroom of the store with the door closed. He was trembling when he picked up the phone to call Jeremy.

"Dude, it's me. Something happened," he said as soon as Jeremy answered.

"What is it?" Jeremy asked.

"I left the backpack on the train. It's gone. The bag is gone."

"*What the fuck?* You left the fucking bag on the train?" Jeremy shouted. "How the fuck could you do something so stupid?" he continued.

"It was an accident. Tash spilled coffee on me and I was distracted and it just happened," Jacob said desperately.

"Tash? What the fuck was she doing there? Does she know what's in the bag?" Jeremy furiously demanded.

"No, no. She was just coming to hang out with me. She doesn't know anything," Jacob said, but Jeremy suspected he was lying. "She told me to call the train station and see if they found the bag. Do you think I should do that? Maybe we can get it back," Jacob said.

"Yeah, that sounds fucking great. Call and ask for the backpack filled with drugs. Have you lost your fucking mind?" Jeremy bellowed.

"Well I just thought maybe they wouldn't have opened it," Jacob said. "You know, like a privacy thing."

"Are you fucking kidding me? You gonna take that chance? Ten to one someone reported a backpack on the train, and the goddamn bomb squad is down there."

"What do we do, man?" Jacob pleaded.

"Let me think. Just let me think for a minute." The only sound Jacob heard was his own labored breathing. Finally, Jeremy said, "Look, we have a few weeks. We have a few weeks to figure it out. Let's not do anything. Just work at the store today, and we can figure it later."

"Ok, ok," Jacob agreed, still trembling.

"And don't fucking bring that bitch back with you, got it?" Jeremy said sternly.

"Yeah, ok," Jacob said. They hung up and Jacob sat in silence, trying to will the room to stop spinning.

*

Jacob persuaded Tash to spend the night at her place, but it wasn't easy and she was pissed. He spent the day running through different scenarios of how this would all play out. He was able to convince himself that it would be all right. Everyone was entitled to a freebie, and this was theirs. It would be ok. That night when he got back to his apartment, Jeremy wasn't there. He waited in the living room for hours. Then, finally ready to go to bed, he walked past Jeremy's bedroom and had a frightening flash. He opened the door, and to his horror, the room was empty. It had been entirely cleared out. He opened the closet and every drawer, but there was no sign of Jeremy, no sign that he had ever been there. He just stood there wondering what he had done, what he had gotten himself into, and what he should do now.

Jacob spent the next three days getting stoned. At one point, he bumped into Melville in the kitchen. Melville asked why he wasn't at work and Jacob told him, "It's none of your fucking business." Tash was texting and calling incessantly, but he didn't respond to her either. He kept thinking that he had a month to figure it out. He just needed to stay put and think.

Then one day, he received a phone call on the landline. It went straight to the machine and he heard Jeremy's voice say, "Pick up the phone."

He flew off the couch and stumbled to the phone. "Hello? Hello? Dude, Jeremy, is that you?"

"Listen, you gotta get out of there."

"What do you mean? Where are you dude? Why'd you take off?" Jacob pleaded.

"Listen, you gotta get out of there."

"But we have four weeks, we have four weeks to figure this out," Jacob said.

"They watch the store. They know you haven't been there. They know there was no delivery. I don't know when they'll come looking, but it'll be soon. You gotta get out of there."

"But ... but we can explain. Can't we explain what happened and ask for a break or something? We can, like, pay it back or something, right?" Jacob asked frantically.

"You gotta get out of there," Jeremy said one last time before hanging up.

Jacob was motionless, holding the dead phone line with ringing in his ears. He could feel his blood coursing through his body but his mind was stuck. He was completely frozen. He hung up the phone, walked over to the couch, and searched for his cell. He sent Tash a text message: "NEED 2 C U PRONTO. ON MY WAY."

He didn't wait for a reply before he grabbed a duffle bag and threw some random clothes and CDs in. He took an envelope of cash he had stashed under his mattress and left.

*

When Jacob arrived at Tash's dorm, he was in such a full-fledged panic that he could barely stop shaking. The desperation and terror in his eyes was the only reason Tash opened the door and let him in. She had planned to leave him out in the hallway begging to come in, only to be rejected. She spent the last few days livid at him, in such a bad way that she had not showered, left the dorm, or eaten anything more substantial than chips from the vending machine. She was strung out and pissed off at her boyfriend – a bad combination. But despite her mental state and her usually reliable preoccupation with herself, she took one look at Jacob, grabbed his hand, and pulled him into her room.

"What the hell is going on?" she asked while hugging him.

He pulled away and sat on her bed. "Where's your roommate?" he asked as he pulled a packet of cigarettes out of his pocket and tried to light one with trembling hands. (It took three matches before he was able to light it.)

"She's away; she's away somewhere for Spring Break. I told you that. Everyone is fucking away. I've been stuck here like a loser," she said as she sat down on the bed opposite Jacob. "You can't smoke in here. The Gestapo will come in and, like, throw me out or something," she continued.

"I thought you said everyone was away," he said anxiously while exhaling a big cloud of smoke.

"Yeah but like there are sprinklers or some shit, and some RA prick. You just can't, you just can't smoke here," she said rubbing her eyes.

He took another deep drag and then dropped the burning cigarette into a nearby Diet Coke can. It made a sizzling sound as the cigarette hit the flat soda.

Tash sat down next to Jacob. He put his head on her shoulder and softly said, "I need to crash here for a while, ok?"

"Yeah, ok. My roommate is coming back soon, I think tomorrow or the next day. Jacob, what's going on?"

"Nothing, I just need to stay here and figure some stuff out, ok?"

"Tell me what's going on. You're really freaking me out," she fumed. "And I'm still mad at you for ditching me."

There was a long pause, and Jacob started to cry. Tash was taken aback. Despite the fact that she was clearly ill-equipped to help anyone, she tried. She rubbed his back and in a much milder tone said, "It's ok. Whatever it is, it's ok. Tell me what's going on." And so he did. He told her everything.

They spent the next twenty-four hours brainstorming. Tash thought that maybe it wouldn't be so bad if he just went back to his apartment and then back to work. He could act as though he didn't know anything about it. When he refuted that idea, she suggested that he could explain what happened and work something out with whomever the drugs belonged to. She offered to try to get some money from her parents. She promised him that she was good at coming up with reasons for them to send money. He didn't think she could possibly get enough. She wanted to call Kyle for help, she trusted him, but Jacob made her swear up and down that she wouldn't tell a soul. By the next night, he was convinced that he needed to get out of town. But as they were falling asleep in her small bed, she muttered, "What about your brother?"

Jacob hadn't even realized that he had left Melville in the apartment. "Shit," he said. "Shit, I forgot about him. I was so fucked when I was leaving."

"Call him, tell him he needs to get out of there," Tash whispered.

"He won't answer the phone," Jacob said.

"Doesn't he have a cell or email or something?" Tash asked.

"No, he doesn't have anything and I told him to never answer the apartment phone." He paused and thought for a moment. "I'll try, I'll try in the morning. I'll shout into the machine and maybe he'll pick up."

Tash and Jacob didn't wake up until two in the afternoon the next day. Groggy and out of it, it took Jacob nearly an hour to remember that he needed to call his brother. He called the apartment at least half a dozen times, screaming into the machine for Melville to pick up, but he never answered. Melville was in the city, hanging out with Pete at the teahouse.

"Shit," Jacob muttered to himself.

Tash came out of her bathroom in a white robe with a towel around her hair. "It feels good to be clean," she said before noticing how distressed Jacob looked. "What is it?" she asked.

"I can't get a hold of Melville. I called like a million times but he won't answer. I knew he wouldn't. Fuck! Fuck!" he screamed. "Hey, don't worry about it," Tash said, walking over to comfort him. "I'm sure he'll be fine. He didn't do anything, and he doesn't know anything. Don't freak out about it."

"I can't just leave him there, Tash. I mean, I can't just fucking leave him there. I don't know what's gonna happen," Jacob said, holding his head in his hands.

"Well, what do you want to do?" she asked as she towel dried her long hair.

"I gotta go back to the apartment, just to tell him to get out of there," Jacob replied.

"Are you sure that's a good idea?" Tash asked.

"There's nothing else I can do. I'll go there and watch the building to make sure there's no one weird hanging around and I'll go in fast and tell him to get out."

Without hesitation Tash said, "I'll go with you."

"No, absolutely not."

"I'm going with you. I have a bunch of stuff in your apartment. Besides, no one's gonna do anything to a girl. I'd be a good lookout or distraction or whatever if you need it."

Jacob was too worked up to think clearly, so he just said, "Ok, ok you can come, but we've gotta be fast. We're not gonna spend time packing all your stuff."

"Fine, I'll just grab my things while you get your brother. We'll be in and out in five minutes," Tash assured him.

*

Melville met Pete at the teahouse at eleven o'clock that morning. They drank coffee and Melville listened to Pete go on and on about an exhibit at the MOMA that he just "must see." They grabbed a quick bite for lunch at a local deli where, as usual, they squabbled over the bill. Melville wanted to pay only for his tuna sandwich, and Pete wanted to split the bill down the middle. Then Pete said that he had plans and had to leave, so Melville headed back to his apartment by train. When Melville finally got home, he opened the refrigerator and took out a small bottle of Orangina. He flipped the cap off and walked into his bedroom, shutting the door behind him. He put his Orangina on his desk, took off his coat, and slung it over the corner of his chair. He lay down on his couch with his head propped up against the pillow and opened a book he'd retrieved from his desk. He left his shoes on.

He had been reading for about twenty minutes when there was loud knocking on the apartment door. He ignored it, assuming that Jacob or Jeremy would get it. Soon, the knocking turned into banging. Melville dog-eared his page and put the book down on his desk. He knocked on Jacob's door, but when there was no answer, he was sure that Jacob had forgotten his keys and had locked himself out again. He opened the door, expecting his brother. Two large men in black leather jackets shoved him into the apartment. He stumbled backwards but quickly regained his footing. In shock, he just stood there as they closed the door behind them.

"Where is it?" they demanded. "Where the fuck is it?"

Melville just shook his head, having no idea what was going on or what to say.

"Come on guy, don't play stupid. We want our loot, and we want the candy shop open for business."

Melville just stood there shaking his head, which enraged the two men. One said to the other, "Do you believe this guy, playing stupid?" He turned back to Melville. "We want the candy shop open, you got it?"

When Melville didn't respond, the two men walked slowly toward him, forcing him to walk backwards. He fell back onto the round kitchen table, leaning as far back as he could while the two men towered over him. They were going to give him one last warning before they left, but Melville didn't know what was happening or what to expect. He reached backward and grabbed the first thing he could feel, a small bottle top from his Orangina. He lunged forward to jam it in one of the guy's eyes, but failed. He tried to run away. Confused, he ran into his bedroom and attempted to lock the door, but the two men pushed their way in.

One grabbed him and screamed at the top of his lungs, "What the fuck was that? What the fuck is wrong with you?"

Melville tried to push back, which caused the man who was holding him to throw him. As Melville tumbled through the air and over his couch, he had one clear thought: it was finally getting warmer in his little room. He was relieved. As he concluded this thought, he smacked his head on the corner of his desk and fell to the floor, lifeless. Blood poured out of the side of his head.

"Oh fuck, Marv. We were just supposed to get the store back open for business. Now we gotta fucking deal with this mess."

"He fell, he just fell," Marv said, shocked. "Well, let's clean this up and get the hell out of here."

The two men searched the apartment for something they could put Melville's body in. With little to choose from, they took comforters from the two other bedrooms, wrapped Melville up, and headed out. On the way out, Marv said, "We should make this look like a break-in." They broke a couple of chairs, flung the kitchen cabinet doors open, and jimmied the lock to the front door.

An hour later, Jacob and Tash arrived at the apartment. Jacob panicked when he saw the apartment door ajar. He pushed the door open, telling Tash to stay back. He walked in slowly and Tash followed, closing the door behind her. The place was in disarray, but he had left in such a hurry and haze that he thought he might have made the mess himself.

"Mel?" he called softly.

"I'll go grab some stuff from your room," Tash said.

"Mel?" Jacob said a little louder. He knocked on the door to Melville's room, and then twisted the knob. He slowly opened the door, hoping to find his brother lying on his couch with his earphones on. "Oh my God," he screamed, seeing the blood all over the desk. He ran over and saw a small pool of blood on the floor too. "Oh my God, oh my God. What have I done? What have I done?" he repeated over and over again. Tash rushed in and Jacob fell to his knees. "Look! Look at this. Oh my God," Jacob continued, now crying and rocking back and forth on the ground.

"Oh shit, Jacob," Tash said in a panic. "We gotta go. We gotta get out of here."

Jacob was inconsolable, so Tash put her hands on his face and forced him to look at her. "We've got to get the fuck out of here. Now Jacob, now."

"But … but, maybe we should call the police or, or …" Jacob had no words.

"What? Are you going to tell them what you think happened?" Tash paused. "Jacob, we don't even know what did happen. Maybe it looks worse than it is. And there's nothing you can do for him now. We've got to get out of here."

Wiping the tears from his face, he nodded.

"I'm gonna get my stuff from your room, and I'll try to grab some of your things too. You can't come back here, not ever. Maybe you should see if there's anything else you really need," she said as she left the room.

Jacob stared at the blood and then decided to take some of Melville's things in case Tash was right; Melville was all right. He grabbed a small milk crate from under Melville's desk, flipped it over, and put some things in it. He chose a stack of notebooks, some loose papers, and a few CDs from the desk. Then he went into his room and threw a jacket with a bag of weed in one of the pockets on top of the crate. Tash was standing with some clothes flung over one of her arms and a small backpack overflowing with Jacob's things. They took what they had and left the apartment in silence.

*

On the train back, Jacob sat with the crate on his lap, unable to control his shaking. Tash tried to comfort him by rubbing his shoulder, but he barely noticed. As they approached the city, Tash asked, "What are you going to do?"

"I've got to get out of here. I'm going to call Mel's best friend, Pete, and see if I can leave Mel's stuff with him just in case Mel is ok and comes back. But I've got to get out of here."

"Do you want to stay with me for a while until you figure things out?" Tash asked.

He shook his head. "I've got to get out of New York for a while." Tash didn't respond, but the look on her face showed that she understood. "Do me a favor," Jacob said as he turned to face her. "Will you look through the papers in here and see if you can find one with a guy named Pete's phone number?" he asked, holding out the crate.

"Sure." She put the crate on her lap. A minute later, she handed Jacob a coffee shop napkin with Pete's name and phone number scribbled on it.

"Thanks," Jacob muttered as he stuffed the napkin in his pants pocket and took the crate back. "I'll get off with you. Then I'm going to call this guy from a payphone and see if he can take this stuff."

"If he can't, I can keep it for you. Maybe you'll come back and you'll want to go through it all," Tash said sweetly.

"Thanks babe, but I don't think you should have anything that belongs to me lying around right now."

She nodded.

The train reached their stop. They stood on the crowded street, and Jacob put the crate down to hug Tash. They squeezed each other tightly.

"Look me up when you come back," she whispered to him.

"Yeah, will do. Take care of yourself. Get your stuff together so you don't, so you don't end up like ..."

Tash interrupted, "Yeah, I know." Then she pulled away and gave him one last model pose, throwing her arms up in the air and exclaiming, "New adventures! Don't let the party end!" She blew him a kiss and sauntered off. He picked up the crate, struggling to keep his overloaded backpack from slipping off his shoulder.

CHAPTER 18

Two hours later, Pete met Jacob at a local diner. Pete didn't know what to make of the frantic phone call, but when Jacob insisted they meet to discuss Melville's safety, he agreed. By the time Pete arrived, Jacob had been sitting in a booth beside the milk crate, drinking black coffee loaded with sugar for nearly two hours. The only reason he hadn't been asked to leave was that the place wasn't crowded. Although the two had never met, they recognized each other immediately. Jacob waved Pete over.

"Hey man," he said as he sat down across from Jacob. "Fuck, I know I don't know what you normally look like, but you look like hell, man," Pete said with his characteristic near laugh and no-holds-barred attitude. "So what's this all about? What's wrong with Melville?" Pete asked as he raised his arm to signal the waitress and mouthed the word "coffee."

After taking a few deep breaths, Jacob began. He told Pete everything and begged him not to repeat a word of it. Quite uncharacteristically, Pete sat quietly and mostly just listened. Each time the waitress came to refill their coffee, Jacob stopped talking.
Blown away, Pete could only say, "Wow, wow. That's a mind blow. Poor Melville. I can't believe it."

"I'm getting out of town tonight. I have some of Mel's things here, and I thought I would leave them with you, you know, in case. If that's all right. I don't know what else to do."

"Well, sure, sure you can leave them with me but don't you think you'd be better off leaving it with your cousin? Melville's probably more likely to call him, don't you think?" Pete asked.

Jacob looked puzzled. "We don't have any cousins. What are you talking about?" he asked.

"Your cousin. You know. Melville was always coming into the city to see him. That's how he and I would usually hook up and hang out, after he had visited his cousin. Are you two like step brothers or something?" Pete asked jokingly.

Jacob shook his head. "Dude, I don't know what Mel told you, but we don't have any cousins. Our parents don't have siblings. We don't have any family in New York at all. You must have misheard him or something."

Pete didn't know what to make of it, but he agreed to take Melville's belongings and wished Jacob good luck.

*

Prilly was just getting home from work when she heard her phone ringing. She let the machine get it but stopped in her tracks at the sound of Pete's voice. She knew she had the willpower to resist the urge to pick up the phone. If she did it once, she could do it again. But when Pete said that something really awful had happened to Melville and that he needed to speak with her, she gave in and picked up the phone. He begged her to come to his apartment. When she refused, he told her he thought Melville was dead and that he needed her. "Please, please Prill, please come over." She agreed. She changed into tight, dark blue jeans and a flowing, gray baby-doll top, fixed her makeup, and took a cab to his apartment. She arrived an hour after he had called.

She was excited, nervous, and unsure of what she was doing. Her hands trembled as she rang the buzzer. As she approached his apartment, the scene of so many heartbreaking and exhilarating moments, he opened the door, gave her a closed-mouthed smile, and said, "Come on in," in his sexiest voice. She sat on the chair by his desk and watched him open a bottle of wine in the kitchen.

"I think I remember you liked Chianti, right?" he asked.

"Actually, I like Cabernet," Prilly said.

"Oh, that's right," he said blushing. "Well this is fabulous. You'll love it. I'm sure it's better than what you normally have."

"Pete, what's going on? I didn't come for a social call. You said Melville might be dead. Were you exaggerating? What are you talking about? What do you mean *might*?"

He handed her a glass and then sat on his bed and took a sip from his own glass. He then told her about the call from Melville's brother, everything Jacob told him, and how he has a box full of

Melville's things, just in case. Prilly couldn't believe it. It was just too awful. She suddenly felt very ashamed of how she had treated Melville; she had always suspected he had a little crush on her.

As Prilly tried to process all of this shocking information, Pete got up and went to the closet. He took out a crate, which he placed on the bed. "That's it. Those are his things. Not much really, poor guy."

"May I?" Prilly asked, indicating she wanted to look in the box.

"Be my guest," Pete said.

As Prilly flipped through the papers (notes about book titles, flyers to local events, some backdated unpaid bills), Pete said, "You know, the weirdest part is something Jacob said to me. He said Melville didn't have any cousins, but that's why he always told me he was in the city. I would bump into him at the teahouse, and he'd tell me he had come into the city to see his cousin. I don't get it," he said shaking his head and taking another sip of wine.

"He was coming to see you. He must have been coming to see you and he felt embarrassed or something to say so," Prilly instantly said, now flipping through his notebooks and remembering how she had once seen him writing in one.

"Wow, you think so? Jeez. What a mindfuck. That's kind of sweet but also really sad, don't you think?" Pete asked.

"I don't know, I guess so," Prilly said. "Have you looked through these? It looks like he was writing a book or something," she continued, holding up one of the notebooks.

Pete shook his head. "I can't imagine it's very good," he said with a laugh. "I know it's terrible to say now, but Melville didn't have an original thought in his life. That's probably why he was so fascinated with me."

"Uh, huh," Prilly said, captivated by what she was reading and wanting to tell Pete he was a jerk.

"Listen, Prilly," Pete said, trying to get her attention, "I've missed you. I've missed you a lot and I think …"

Prilly didn't let him finish. "Pete, please. Don't. I only came because you said something horrible happened to Melville. Don't read anything else into it. I can't go there again."

"Ah, but you wouldn't have come if you didn't still have feelings for me. You know it's true. So it's silly to be stubborn about it …"

"Pete, I'm going to go. You seem ok and I'm not going to do this with you. I'm not. I just can't." She got up and turned to leave. Then she paused and turned back to face Pete. "What are you going to do with those things?"

"I don't know. I guess I'll just stick them in the closet," he said, shrugging his shoulders.

"Well if you're just going to do that, do you mind if I take the notebooks? I'd like to read what he wrote. I can send them back to you if you want."

"Sure, sure, you can take them," Pete said. "You'll be disappointed, my dear, but suit yourself. Keep 'em."

Prilly removed the notebooks from the crate and headed to the front door. Pete followed her and put his hand out, shutting the door before she could walk out. She turned around, pressed firmly between Pete and the door. He leaned in to kiss her, but she turned her head. He pulled back, rejected. "I really hope Melville turns up and that he's all right," she said. Then she walked out of the apartment.

During the cab ride home, she experienced a slew of emotions. She felt sad for Melville, vindicated that Pete still wanted her, and both pride and pain at having to walk away. More than ever, the things he said and the way he said them showed her that he wasn't capable of caring about anyone except for himself. She knew that would never work for her. He was so arrogant, and for once, looking around that dingy little apartment, she couldn't quite figure out why. That night, she lay on her couch reading Melville's notebooks, which were a mix of memoir and fantasy with some mindless ramblings interspersed throughout. But there was a story in it all. It was a story about a shy and lonely man who longed to be all that he wasn't. She found it quite beautiful.

*

The next morning, Janice was brewing her decaf when Kyle came into the kitchen to grab an energy drink. "You're up early," she said, surprised to see him.

"Yeah, I'm meeting a friend for breakfast before school."

"Oh," Janice said, as she poured a cup of coffee. "Well, don't be late for school."

"Don't worry. I have a study hall first period."

"Who are you meeting? Sam?" she asked before taking her first sip of coffee.

"No, just a friend who was having some problems. She is better now, I think, and I'm just checking up on her."

"That's nice honey," Janice said. "Kyle," she called, as he was halfway through the dining room.

"Yeah Mom?" he paused and asked.

"It's nice how you look out for your friends. It's very nice. My mother is like that. That's all … I just wanted to say that."

Kyle walked back to her and gave her a kiss on her forehead. He smiled and left, hollering, "Have a great day," before shutting the front door.

She enjoyed another sip of her coffee and then noticed her Blackberry was vibrating in her suit pocket. She took it out and scrolled to her new emails. There was one from Prilly that read: "Janice: On my way to pick up the posters. See you at the convention center. Prilly."

Janice slipped her Blackberry into her pocket, leaned against the kitchen counter, and finished her coffee while admiring the ivory molding that framed the kitchen doorway.

AFTERWORD

Low-Fat Love was a secret project. The only person who knew about it was Mark, the man I married within days of finishing the first draft. Initially, I was writing it for myself, to make sense of what I had learned from my interviewees, students, and friends over the years. I longed to get my ideas and perspective out, uncensored. I also needed to process my own past relationships. Writing has always been my path. I had no idea if I would finish it, nor had any plans to publish it. As I progressed, I felt that I was no longer just writing for myself. By the time it was finished, Mark and I agreed that I should seek publication.

I explored various avenues for publishing, including seeking a literary agent to publish it as a traditional novel, self-publishing, and working with an academic publisher. While *Low-Fat Love* is a novel that can be read by anyone as a beach read, it also embodies many years of my research and teaching experiences. I have always considered the novel a piece of arts-based research, and ultimately wanted it published as such. I didn't know how to build a bridge between the world of academic publishing and what appeared on the surface as a piece of chick lit, better suited for a commercial press. Eventually I came up with the idea for a book series that would house my novel, as well as the research-informed novels, plays, and short story collections of others. The idea for the *Social Fictions* book series was born. Fortunately, Peter de Liefde, owner of Sense Publishers, leaders in educational book publishing, agreed to give the series a chance. Neither of us could have predicted the incredible journey that partnership would produce. Most recently, we were elated when I received a Special Achievement Award from the American Creativity Association for the *Social Fictions* series, which they called groundbreaking.

Writing and sharing *Low-Fat Love* was a healing process for me. I certainly settled for low-fat love and suffered from self-esteem issues when I was younger. My experience of choosing a creative path arose from personal pain and professional frustration. Walking that path with others has been enriching beyond words. The response to *Low-Fat Love* has been humbling. Both women and men have stopped me after book talks and conference presentations, or have come to book signings to tell me their own stories, often involving settling in love or life. I am profoundly moved that people have taken the time to share their stories with me, and I am honored that the novel has become a platform for self-reflection. I am changed by these experiences.

As a sociologist and educator, I am enormously grateful that professors across the disciplines have incorporated *Low-Fat Love* into their classes. That's a dream come true, especially in an age in which standardization is pushed. It is heartening to see this kind of engaged teaching and learning practiced. I'm also amazed by the unexpected opportunities the novel has afforded me, from hosting my own radio show called *Low-Fat Love 101* to writing blogs for organizations that I respect, including my blog, "Low-Fat Love 101" for *We Are the Real Deal*. These opportunities, along with the support of readers and Sense Publishers, led to this anniversary edition.

It's interesting how we think of some art forms as open to revision and/or reinterpretation. For example, musicians often put out new versions of their work, such as remastered editions, live versions, or orchestral reinterpretations. Likewise, director's cuts of films often significantly alter the original narrative. Other forms, like novels, are presented as static. Perhaps this is because the textual form of words on a page, literally in black and white, seems less malleable. New editions of novels often just mean a new, more contemporary cover, or a new foreword.

I took this anniversary edition on, in part, to show that literary forms are also alive and open to re-imaginings. I must admit that the writer in me was terrified to go back and read the novel years after writing it. I knew it was flawed. While I am proud of the novel in its original form, as it was the best I was able to do at the time, part of me had hoped for a do-over. There's a limit to what you can revise in a novel that many people have already read, but the book needed a good copyediting and other refinements. I think of this revised and expanded anniversary edition as similar to releasing a digitally remastered album. My hope is that it is simply a better version of itself. I must say I did also find the task of going back to revise the novel daunting. As I expected, I found many embarrassing errors and areas that could be strengthened. However, the process also made me more appreciative of the original. I see more in it now than when I first wrote it. I actually think I'm better able to understand what I was doing now because there is distance. At the time, writing was such an emotional process of working through years of personal and professional experiences. I just did it, but I couldn't properly process what I was doing. The novel held a space to grow and to accommodate my growth. So I want to thank Peter de Liefde for the opportunity to go back and ultimately form a new and stronger relationship with the book.

Whether you have come to this version with fresh eyes or after having read the original, I hope you're able to take something from it. In more ways than one, this novel has been a great gift to me, and as strange as it may sound, I am enormously grateful to the characters that live on its pages.

As a part of the anniversary edition, I am happy to include bonus material. First, I share and respond to the comments and questions posed by readers like you from around the world. Also included are some of the ways professors are using the novel in their classrooms.

Love and Light,
Patricia

Q&A

I've been deeply fortunate to speak with readers at universities, conferences, and book events. Readers have made fascinating observations about the novel and how certain aspects have resonated with their own experiences. I have also been asked many questions, some repeatedly. So here are some of the most common comments and questions I've heard, as well as my responses.

1. Explain the title.

Low-fat love is a concept. It's like love-lite. It's about settling for less than we really want and trying to pretend it's better than it is. It's the idea of accepting butter substitute in place of butter and trying to pretend it's the real thing. When it comes to food, there may be health benefits to settling for a substitute, but when it comes to relationships, including the relationship we have with ourselves, there is no substitute for the real deal. Faking it never works.

2. What's with the doughnuts (on the original cover)?

The idea was to take something that looks appealing on the surface but isn't good for us. If you binge on a box of doughnuts, you probably won't feel that great afterward. Of all pastries, I thought doughnuts were perfect because they have a hole in the center, as if something is missing.

3. Pop culture comes up throughout the book. Can you talk about the pop culture references?

Pop culture plays a significant role in the book as the subtext. Every reference was selected with intent. For example, the movies Janice watches before she goes to Detroit are both about how you can't erase or cover up the truth. Even the selection of the play, *Wicked*, which Janice is briefly said to have taken Tash to, carries meaning. I spent a long time deciding which play to mention there. The references are subtle at times, but they are important. More explicitly, I used women's media as a signpost throughout the book in order to make visible the context in which women come to think of themselves, as well as the men and women in their lives. As a feminist sociologist, I attempted to offer a critical commentary about popular culture and the social construction of femininity. For instance, Prilly is repeatedly engaged in consuming media targeted at women, such as tabloid TV, home shopping, Lifetime movies, plays, books, and even music videos. The sociologist in me was trying to link the macro context with people's individual, micro-level experiences. So media culture (the macro level) impacts Prilly personally (the micro level). I also used pop culture to mirror what was going on with the characters. For example, Prilly makes two purchases from Home Shopping. One item isn't as advertised but she tries to pretend it is better than it is. She decides she loves the other item only when she receives a compliment from a rival coworker. In these instances, Prilly's purchases are used to mirror her two major relationship mistakes: settling for less than she really wants and pretending it's better than it is, and seeking external validation to feel good about herself. Some readers have told me they read the book more than once to tease out the meanings of the pop culture references.

4.   The Prilly and Pete question. Who is really at fault?

From doing talks about *Low-Fat Love*, I've come to see that there are two schools of thought on the topic of Prilly and Pete. Some readers think Pete is a total jerk and treated Prilly horribly, but others think that Prilly was to blame for participating in the melodramatic relationship. Both interpretations are equally valid, as are others one may come up with. When I was writing the book, I wanted to call readers' attention to their own individual choices. At the end of the day, we can only work on ourselves. My friends and the women I've interviewed have said things like, "I have such bad luck with men." My response is always, "Uh, no. You make your own luck." I know I did. In other words, we have to take some responsibility for how we feel about ourselves, what expectations we bring to our relationships, and our own decisions to participate in relationships with people who withhold or otherwise can't give us what we really want. For me, the most important thing was for Prilly to recognize her own role in what was clearly a destructive relationship and to make better choices going forward. There's no doubt that at a minimum, Pete exacerbates Prilly's insecurities. But is he responsible for them?

5.   Janice's father doesn't have a name. Why is that?

It was very challenging to write the scenes in Janice's family home, which were mostly dialogue, without naming that character. I did this intentionally because I felt that her father had such a large and overwhelming presence in her identity that I didn't want to give him more power with a name. Similarly, because Prilly is so preoccupied with her physical appearance, I never describe what she looks like beyond a brief description of her hair. It's funny because I've had countless people tell me at book readings that I do describe what Prilly looks like, before conceding that, in fact, they had just imagined her so clearly. I did this for two primary reasons. First, beauty is in the eye of the beholder. It doesn't matter what she looks like; what matters is how she feels about herself and her appearance. Second, I wanted female readers who may identify with Prilly to see themselves in her.

6.   Janice was a horrible person but I also kind of felt badly for her.

Many readers have told me that they felt conflicted because they perceive Janice as a horrible person but they also felt badly about her empty marriage and traumatic childhood. There's no doubt that this character is difficult and I make no excuses for her poor behavior. I wouldn't want her as a colleague or friend. However, I do think that so often people have stories that we know nothing of, and many struggle in silence. We all have our own demons to confront and it is only when we do that honestly and authentically that we can have a healthy relationship with ourselves and hopefully with others. Janice has only just begun that process.

7.   Kyle seems different than the other characters.

Because the strongest male characters in the book are negative forces, it was important to have a positive male character for balance. Arguably, Kyle is the most positive character in the book. If I were going to pick someone to be friends with or to emulate, it would be him. I will share something personal about how I decided to write this character. Part Two opens with a long description of Kyle that was actually a secret love letter to my daughter, Madeline. She was much younger than Kyle at the time, and she's a girl, so I want to be clear that she is not him. I simply took some of her best qualities and even a couple of sparks of truth from her life to initially develop that character.

8. Was Tash sexually assaulted at the New Year's Eve party?

We only have what is on the written page so I don't know more than any other reader about what happened behind closed doors. I do have my personal beliefs about what happened, but I'll leave it up to readers to decide.

9. Charles Pruit's suicide.

With the exception of Kyle, I see the characters as isolated and lonely. Even Tash, for me, represents another version of insecurity. Insecurity can be a lonely place. I think it's important to be honest about where loneliness, disappointment, and rejection, perhaps coupled with depression, can potentially lead. Suicide comes up twice in the book, first with Charles and then with Janice's father. Many of the characters are staring down a rabbit hole, and this is one extreme version of where that rabbit hole can sadly lead. Prilly identifies with both Charles and Melville. While I didn't want the protagonist to meet the fate of either of those characters, I did want to show another possibility for someone who suffers in silence and isolates him or herself. What happens to Charles could easily have happened to Prilly, or for that matter, Janice. The path was possible.

10. Melville.

Melville was my favorite character to write and serves a couple of roles in the novel. First, I believe that when a person doesn't find their voice, they disappear. I wanted to find a way to make Melville actually, physically disappear; he became a metaphor for what happens to people who don't find themselves. Melville and Prilly have a lot in common. Both are drawn to Pete despite how he treats them, and neither is able to say aloud how they are really feeling. Neither has found their voice. Throughout the novel, I only represent the interiority of these two characters so that readers can see, through their interior dialogue, how they actually feel about themselves. Second, Melville suffers the consequences for all of the characters. Each character put him or herself in situations that could have dire consequences, including creating financial debt, losing one's job, contracting a sexually transmitted disease, or overdosing. Of course, not all of the characters will suffer the potential consequences of their actions, so Melville represents what *could* happen.

11.   I thought Melville and Prilly would end up together.
The most important relationship Prilly has is with herself, and that was the one she needed to work on. I also intended to subvert the traditional chick lit narrative that has the protagonist end up with the guy, or even "the other" guy.

12.   The ending.
It's funny because I wrote the kind of ending that I've always had a problem with in books and movies, and I completely accept that it may be disappointing to some readers. However, now I understand why artists go for those open endings. *Low-Fat Love* was intended to mirror daily life. For example, there are many scenes in which we see people engaged in their daily habits, in the monotony of everyday life. Scenes like these are important in order to understand these characters' choices and attitudes, to understand the gap between their dreams and their realities. We need to know what their daily lives are really like. It's a part of the sociology of the book. In life, there aren't big endings in the middle of our stories, and people typically don't radically change who they are, at least not overnight. I think the best we can hope for is gradual growth. That's a realistic benchmark. So that's where I left these characters on their journeys.

13.   What has been the most surprising response to the novel?
Right after it was released, a woman approached me in a hallway to ask me if the novel was about her. I hardly knew a thing about this

woman, so it certainly was not based on her. I giggled a bit when she was surprised with my answer. Since then, I've received this kind of comment in many different ways, including people saying things like, "You wrote my life." It's always a huge compliment.

14.   Will there be a sequel?

No, at least not in the traditional sense. I look at *Low-Fat Love* as a character study and I think I have fully explored the main characters with respect to how their lives relate to one another. I don't see the material for a sequel, nor do I have the desire. However, that doesn't mean I won't someday take one or two of the lesser explored characters and write their stories. I am also working on a project that is inspired by the stories women have shared with me since *Low-Fat Love* came out. I was so deeply affected by women's stories of settling and disappointment that I conducted new interviews explicitly on those themes. Those interviews are the basis for a new project I am working on. It's called *Low-Fat Love Stories* because it was inspired by the stories that were inspired by the novel. For the first time in my career, I've been collaborating with a visual artist and hope the book project will be multimedia or have multiple outcomes.

CLASSROOM USE

1.   *Low-Fat Love* is, in many ways, a book about self-esteem. What are some examples of this in the book? What are the self-esteem issues the characters encounter – Prilly, Janice, Tash, Melville – and how do those issues shape their experiences?

2.   *Low-Fat Love* explores the psychology of negative relationships through a focus on the "inner worlds" of characters. Explore this topic using any of the following relationships: Prilly and Pete, Janice and her family, Janice and Richard, Tash and Kyle.

3.   The use of fiction allows for the exploration of the "inner worlds" of characters through techniques such as interior monologue. How did this technique help to get at the deep issues of self-esteem and identity the characters were struggling with?

4.   Many of the characters in *Low-Fat Love* are attracted to people who withhold their support (Prilly to Pete; Prilly to Janice; Melville to Pete; Janice to her father). Explore this issue.

5.   The storyline surrounding Janice and her trip home to confront her demons deals with how alcoholism can create a dysfunctional family system, and how different people within the family system cope with the situation. Discuss these issues. Further, how is gender at play in these family dynamics?

6.   The storyline surrounding Tash – the college party-girl – explores the patterns of destructive behaviors that college students sometimes engage in. What were Tash's motivations and how are we to make sense of this character? How are these issues reflected on your college campus?

7.   What are the body image issues that manifest in the book? How does poor body image shape Prilly's experiences? What is the media context in which she developed her body image?

8.   Pop culture, particularly women's media, is used as a sign post throughout the book to show the larger context in which women build their identities and live out their lives. In the book, what picture is painted of women's pop culture? How do you think this impacted the characters? (You can highlight all of the pop culture references in the book and jot down your ideas of the "pop culture world" they painted.)

CREATIVE WRITING ASSIGNMENTS

1.   Select one of the minor characters and write his/her story.

2.   Select one of the characters and fast-forward five years. Write a short story based on where you think they are now.

3.   Pick a scene written in the narrator's voice and rewrite it using interior dialogue and/or dialogue.

4.   Pick a scene written in the narrator's voice and rewrite it with one of the main characters, either Prilly or Janice, as the narrator.

5.   Write an alternative ending to *Low-Fat Love*.

SMALL GROUP ACTIVITIES

1.   Student groups of 3-5 explore the following question prior to reading *Low-Fat Love*:

What is an unhealthy relationship?

When the class has finished reading *Low-Fat Love,* groups reconvene to explore the following question:

After reading *Low-Fat Love,* conduct a group discussion and revise your response to the original question, "What is an unhealthy relationship?"

2.   Student groups of 3-5 explore the question:

Low-Fat Love can be used to explore the social construction of femininity and masculinity. Have a discussion about how the characters in the book illustrate some of the ways we construct and perform gender identities. All groups then reconvene and share their ideas. Keep notes on the blackboard, creating one column for femininity and one for masculinity. This activity can be changed to explore the primary agents of socialization (peers, media) and how they influence our identity-development processes.

QUALITATIVE RESEARCH ACTIVITIES

1.   Select several scenes and perform discourse or conversation analysis on the dialogue or interior dialogue. For example, use the scene in which Janice has lunch with her friend Sarah Cohen, Janice and Prilly's lunch at Nico's, or the conversation about love and relationships between Prilly and Pete at the diner.

2.   Conduct a content analysis of the pop-culture items and other objects in the book.

ABOUT THE AUTHOR

Patricia Leavy, PhD is an independent scholar and novelist (formerly Associate Professor of Sociology and Founding Director of Gender Studies at Stonehill College). She is widely considered a leader in the fields of arts-based research and qualitative inquiry. Her seventeen published books include *Method Meets Art: Arts-Based Research Practice* (first and second editions) (Guilford Press), *The Oxford Handbook of Qualitative Research* (Oxford University Press), *Fiction as Research Practice: Short Stories, Novels and Novellas* (Left Coast Press), *Essentials of Transdisciplinary Research: Using Problem-Centered Methodologies* (Left Coast Press), and the arts-based novel *American Circumstance* (Sense Publishers). She edits five book series including *Social Fictions, Teaching Gender, Teaching Race & Ethnicity, Teaching Writing* (for Sense Publishers) and *Understanding Qualitative Research* (for Oxford University Press). Known for her commitment to public scholarship, she is frequently called on by the national news media and blogs for *The Huffington Post* and *The Creativity Post*. The New England Sociological Association named her the 2010 New England Sociologist of the Year and she received the prestigious 2014 American Creativity Association Special Achievement Award for her work advancing arts-based research. Please visit her website for more information: www.patricialeavy.com

Printed in the United States
By Bookmasters